THE MEANING OF WORDS.

THE MEANING OF WORDS:

ANALYSED INTO

WORDS AND UNVERBAL THINGS,

AND

UNVERBAL THINGS CLASSIFIED INTO INTELLECTIONS, SENSATIONS, AND EMOTIONS.

BY

A. B. JOHNSON,

AUTHOR OF A "TREATISE ON BANKING," "RELIGION IN ITS RELATION TO THE PRESENT LIFE," ETC., ETC.

Four ineradicable fallacies are concealed in the structure of language: it identifies what unverbally are diverse, assimilates what unverbally are heterogeneous, makes a unit of what unverbally are multifarious, and transmutes into each other what unverbally are untransmutable.

New York:

D. APPLETON AND CO., 443 & 445 BROADWAY.

1862.

TO

ALEXANDER S. JOHNSON,

JUDGE OF THE COURT OF APPEALS,

OF THE STATE OF NEW YORK.

My dear Son,

I believe your recollection can extend back to no period when we were not companions of each other, and I often query which of us is more indebted to the other for intellectual and moral benefits thereby received; but I usually adjudge myself to be the debtor. The topics of this book you have heard from me in every form in which my intellect can conceive them, hence I inscribe the book to you, not to communicate its contents, but to record the social relationship which has always existed between us.

Of the merits of the work neither of us is in a good position to judge—I from self-love, and you from prepossessions towards me. It has, however, exerted a kindly influence over my leisure during a long life that has been marked with sorrows of no ordinary magnitude. It has, indeed, been to me like the poor man's lamb in the parable of the prophet. "It has grown up with me and my children, eaten of my meat, drunk of my own cup, lain in my bosom, and been unto me as a daughter." Praying you may possess a son to whom you may be able to transmit a memorial of social intercourse, like that recorded in this dedication,

I remain yours most faithfully,

THE AUTHOR.

Utica, *State of New York*, 1854.

PREFACE.

The inventor of the "Rule of Three" deemed his object accomplished when he presented sufficient examples of his rule to elucidate its rationale and utility. I, also, have not communicated all the results which will follow from my analysis of language, but rather as few as will suffice to elucidate my doctrines, the materials for the elucidation being taken from any source that seemed to me best adapted to the purpose; and taken usually from my memory irrespective of their merits or demerits for other purposes. Indeed many of the scientific tenets on which I comment are probably no longer authoritative, and my comments may misconceive those which are authoritative, and kindred errors may be numerous; but if the reader shall collect from my comments the views of language that I entertain, he will collect all that I seek to accomplish, and I plead guilty in advance of all the scientific errors of which he may be able to convict me.

Some paintings require to be examined at a distance, others need a near inspection or the merits of the picture cannot be ascertained. What distance of view is to paintings, rapidity of reading is to books. The following sheets are constructed for very slow reading—the slower the better; and whoever reads them fast will be unable to judge accurately of their design, and had better not read at all. I have found a difference myself between reading my speculations in manuscript, and reading them in print,—manuscript being naturally read more slowly than print, and the effect of the difference causes the printed work to be less satisfactory to me than the manuscript.

These pages convey my conceptions neither as fully as I wish, nor as methodically and perspicuously, but they are the miniature results of at least fifty years of reflection, intently directed to a search whose object I at first saw but dimly, and to which I approached by slow approximations. In the year 1828, I published my first views under the title of "The Philosophy of Human Knowledge, or a Treatise on Language." It was published in New York, by G. & C. Carvill. In the year 1836, I rewrote the whole work and it was published in the same city, by Harper & Brothers, under the title of "A Treatise on Language, or the Relation which Words bear to Things." Some years after both these publications, I heard, accidentally, of a work on language somewhat similar in conception to mine. Its author is the late Sir Graves Chamney Haughton, F. R. S., and of the Institute of France, etc., and author of a Bengalee Dictionary and other learned works. He named his production Prodromus, and it was published in London, in the year 1839. Like my above named two publications, it deemed intellectually conceived words as nothing but words, and deemed the ultimate significations of all words to be only sensible perceptions and internal feelings. I suppose such a limitation necessarily precedes the fuller conception of language contained in the present publication; our knowledge being naturally cumulative and progressive.

In some places, I anticipate remarks that are subsequently repeated in places where they more properly belong. I have not been able to avoid this defect without more labour than I thought the defect justified; for I have not duplicated the same matter except to subserve some new purpose. But another difficulty exists that no care can obviate, for it is organic in our intellect. Its rationale will be found in the following sheets where they speak of general propositions:—every modern discovery is subsequently found to be included in some propositions that have descended to us from past ages. Even a foreshadowing of the electric telegraph has been lately seen in the scornful exclamation found in the Book of Job, "Canst thou send lightnings that they may go and say unto thee, here we are!" Like the above, every sentence of a book suggests to the reader something that he knows, while the writer may have intended something that the reader knows not. The difficulty presents an insurmountable obstacle against the direct communication by words of new intellectual conceptions. The most which verbal communications can accomplish in the premises, is by a species of fermentation or elicitation in the reader's intellect, whereby the new doctrines may possibly become evolved, or, as we say, conceived—a term that is more literal than figurative.

But to the above irremediable difficulty in the communicability, by means of words, of new conceptions that are not merely lexicographical definitions, we add an avoidable difficulty of which the following is an example:—"We hold these truths to be self-evident, that all men are created equal." Equal in what?—surely some men are created deaf, some blind, some idiotic, deformed, feeble, black, etc. How self-evidently untrue, therefore, is the above miscalled self-evident truth of our Declaration of Independence! Such criticism is sometimes heard from men in high stations, and it may be philological, but to deem it controversial of the author's meaning is to commit the error I am anxious to expose. The meaning of the declaration is not what it excludes, but what it includes;—not what is false therein, but what is true; and thus interpreted it is a summary of many truths; as, for instance, men are created "not with saddles on their backs," to designate that they are to be ridden, but rather with no peculiar adaptation to the artificial distinctions that men impose on each other. All are created equally subject to the same infections, pains, wounds, mischances, and death; all are created with the same passions, instincts, self-love, and impatience of injury; and though some men are created deaf, blind, idiotic, etc., such evils are dispensed with no reference to artificial social distinctions, but like sunshine and rain fall on all classes indiscriminately.

Sectarian dogmas are preeminently subjected by opposing sectaries to the foregoing captious misinterpretations, hence the incessant criminations and recriminations that painfully disfigure all polemical discussions of men whom we wish to respect; while probably every sectarian tenet is correct in its proper meaning, and every controvertist is combatting a monster of only his own conception. "I will tell you, sir," said Laplace, to one of his friends, "what is the greatest absurdity in the world: it is the doctrine of transubstantiation, for it violates both time and space." I will not venture to say what the doctrine signifies to those who hold it understandingly, but I have no doubt they would indignantly reject any absurdity therefrom that Laplace would imply. In every instance, therefore, where a reader finds that his interpretation of an author contradicts the author's comments and conclusions, the reader should amend his interpretation, and make it conform to the author's comments and conclusions. At least, I crave such an interpretation for my following speculations, if they shall haply gain a reader. We read in vain if we look into a book as we look into a mirror, and receive back nothing but a reflection of our own familiar lineaments. Finally, I could not make the work pleasant to readers who seek amusement only, but I have tried faithfully to make it brief and intelligible, and especially, to make it useful to those who desire a knowledge of the structure of language—a knowledge which bears the same relation to all speculative learning as a knowledge of the qualities of drugs bears to the practice of medicine, or as a knowledge of perspective and colours bears to painting. Persons who know not the latent sophistries of language, know no verbal knowledge unfallaciously, and in proportion as their defect is unsuspected, the world, considered speculatively, will be full of mysteries, and differ from unverbal realities as jugglery differs from ordinary operations. To manifest these truths is, however, not easy. A celebrated English physician deemed a milk diet so healthful, that he said a stomach which cannot endure milk is the stomach most in need of milk; and I will parody the remark, by saying that a man who supposes he has nothing to learn in relation to the structure of language, is probably the man who is most in need of such learning. To show still more strongly my own opinion of the nature of this publication—aside from its execution, of whose many defects I am only too painfully conscious—I believe that a full fruition of what is herein attempted will make no longer true the ancient oracle, which I suppose referred to language, and which was engraven on the pavement of Minerva's temple, "I am all that has been, that is, and that shall be, and none among mortals has hitherto taken off my veil."

CONTENTS.

LECTURE I.—Introductory, Explanatory, and Postulatory.

1. Words are originally unmeaning sounds. Words conceived in thought are not different in this respect from oral words—oral words being only articulated sounds, and words conceived in thought being only inaudible articulations.
2. The meaning of all words is conventional, and can be analysed into a verbal meaning and an unverbal. The unverbal meaning alone is considered by me—indeed, to discriminate the unverbal meaning from the verbal is the main object of the work.
3. The unverbal meaning of words is divisible into three classes—sensible, intellectual, and moral. The class that I call moral is composed of our internal feelings, which latter designation being more indicative of my meaning than the word "moral," I usually employ it in preference to "moral," though I sometimes use the word "emotional."
4. The elements of chemistry are so generically different from each other that no one element can be converted into another. Unverbal things—sensible, intellectual, and emotional—are equally different from each other generically, and equally inconvertible into one another, except verbally, though they seem homogeneous when contemplated through the medium of words.
5. Chemistry is at the end of its analysis when it has resolved physical bodies into the respective generical elements of which the bodies are composed; and our unverbal knowledge is at the end of its analysis when it is resolved into its unverbal generic components, sensible, intellectual, and emotional.
6. Oxygen, and every other chemical element, is its own best expositor. It is what it is—just as God, in addressing Moses from the burning bush, could no way so well designate His personality as by saying, "I am that I am." So its own best expositor is each sensible perception, intellectual conception, and internal feeling. Each is what it is, and to characterise it in any verbal way is to prevent the discrimination of words from unverbal things.
7. The ultimate elements of our unverbal knowledge is not words, but unverbal things—the unverbal meaning underlies the verbal.

8. Every man is dependent on his senses for his unverbal sensible knowledge, and the unverbal knowledge revealed to him by any one of his senses cannot be revealed to him by any one or more of his other senses, the revelations of each sense being unique when estimated unverbally.
9. A man's intellect can yield him no sensible information, the intellect being able to yield intellectual conceptions only.
10. Every nominal thing which is insensible is intellectual, unless it be an internal feeling, and every nominal internal feeling that cannot be felt unverbally is also an intellection only.
11. The words "physical" and "sensible," wherever employed in these pages, are used as synonyms; the words "moral," "emotional," and "internal feelings," are also employed as synonyms of each other.

PART I.

OF THE STRUCTURE OF LANGUAGE.

LECTURE II.—The Heterogeneity of Unverbal Things discriminated from their Fallacious Verbal Homogeneity.

1. We possess but one set of words with which to speak of three inconvertibly different sets of unverbal things.
2. The verbal sameness must be discriminated from the unverbal diversity, or much speculative error ensues.
3. We mistake the homogeneity of words for a characteristic of unverbal things.

LECTURE III.—Unverbal Multiplicity discriminated from its Fallacious Verbal Oneness.

1. Names analysed, and their implied oneness found to be intellectual—verbal, not unverbal.
2. All individuality is a conception of the intellect.
3. The intellect aggregates sensible perceptions into nominal units.
4. The intellect aggregates internal feelings into nominal units.
5. The intellect aggregates its own conceptions into nominal units.
6. The intellect aggregates into nominal units its own conceptions associated with certain internal feelings.

LECTURE IV.—Verbal Identity analysed into Unverbal Diversity.

1. Identity is a subjective conception of the intellect, not an objective perception of the senses.
2. Physical things that are verbally identical, are identical in only the conception of the intellect.
3. Intellectual things that are verbally identical, are identical in only the conception of the intellect.

4. Internal feelings which are verbally identical, are identical in only the conception of the intellect.
5. Language is founded on the two intellectual organic processes of creating nominal units and verbal identities.

PART II.

OF THE INTERPRETATION OF WORDS.

LECTURE V.—Of the Unverbal Signification of Words.

1. The verbal identity of any two or more unverbal things must be interpreted by their unverbal diversity.
2. The verbal homogeneity of any two or more words must be interpreted by their unverbal heterogeneity.
3. The verbal oneness of any verbal thing must be interpreted by its unverbal multiplicity.

LECTURE VI.—Of the Unverbal Interpretation of Affirmative General Propositions.

1. The generality of a proposition is subjective, and refers to the intellect; but the objective signification of a proposition is governed by the unverbal objects to which it refers.
2. Every general proposition possesses as many different objective significations, as it refers to different objects.

LECTURE VII.—Of the Unverbal Meaning of Negative General Propositions.

1. A negation that refers to no physical object is physically insignificant.
2. The absence of a physical negative will make an affirmative proposition true universally; yet the proposition will mean affirmatively only the sensible particulars to which its affirmation refers.

LECTURE VIII.—Of the Unverbal Interpretation of Words that are Intellectually Conceived.

1. Words conceived by the intellect mean, unverbally, the organism of the intellect; not the objects which the words mean when they apply to perceptions of the senses.
2. Intellectually conceived words are organic subjective responses of the intellect to objective premises.
3. As a man increases his objective knowledge, he increases the materials out of which his intellect conceives its subjective verbal responses.
4. The intellect cannot originate objective knowledge, except what relates to its own organism.
5. The responses of the intellect are independent of our volition.

LECTURE IX.—The Same Subject Continued.

1. The subjective nature of intellectual verbal conceptions, as contradistinguished from objective things, is urged upon our notice by the necromantic dilemmas to which the intellect organically arrives in predicating such conceptions to their ultimate results.
2. Conceptions of the intellect are organic, but not innate, their evolvement depending on accidental objective occurrences.

LECTURE X.—Of the Unverbal Meaning of Verbal Inquisition.

1. Retrospect of the preceding lectures.
2. Questions analysed into an inquirer, inquiree, and object.
3. Each of the three is unverbally triform, and only verbally a unit.
4. The error exemplified of seeking sensibly what is only intellectual, and seeking intellectually what is only sensible.
5. Inquisition is limited by the purview of our sensible, intellectual, and moral organisms.
6. All physical inquisition is unanswerable that is not within the purview of the senses, all intellectual inquisition is unanswerable that is not within the purview of the intellect, and all inquisition that relates to the internal feelings is unanswerable that is not within the purview of our consciousness therein.
7. Knowledge, except of language, is, in its ultimate form, not verbal, but unverbal.
8. Conclusion.

CAUTION TO THE HASTY READER.

A table of contents being necessarily composed of general propositions, is, in a work like the present, as unintelligible, when not preceded by the items in detail to which the general propositions refer, as a catalogue of plants is unintelligible to a person unacquainted with the plants. This has prevented me from making as copious as I otherwise should the above table, and the headings which precede each lecture. The table and headings but glance at some of the main topics of the work, and omit wholly collateral reflections and consequences, which as necessarily accompany the main topics of every work as foliage accompanies the production of fruit.

THE MEANING OF WORDS.

LECTURE I.

INTRODUCTORY AND EXPLANATORY.

CONTENTS.

1. Words signify either words or unverbal things.
2. Unverbal things are either sensible, intellectual or emotional.
3. The unverbal things of any one of the above three classes are untransmutable into the unverbal things of any other of the classes except verbally.
4. The unverbal things of the different classes seem homogeneous when contemplated through the medium of words.

§ 1. Like the whistle of the winds, the lowing of oxen, and the chirp of birds, words are mere sounds, apart from the signification which they acquire conventionally or otherwise; and to the people of one nation, the unaccustomed language of another nation is still unmeaning sounds. Words, whenever used significantly, must, therefore, signify other words or unverbal things, or both; but so far as words signify other words, I shall not discuss their meaning, how important soever the verbal meaning of words may be; for it constitutes a branch of learning which has been abundantly cultivated, and I can add nothing thereto. I design to speak of only the unverbal signification of words,—the signification which no explanatory words can reach, it underlying them all.

§ 2. I shall not, however, attempt to establish the unverbal meaning of any particular word, but simply attempt to discriminate words from unverbal things;—the discrimination applying to all words in common, and to all languages. The meaning of particular words, as matter, spirit, body, mind, etc., is constantly engaging the efforts of philosophers, who suppose they are engaged in profounder discussions than merely defining the signification of particular words;—but I disclaim the discussion, not because I deem it unimportant, but because the disclaimer will aid in showing, by contrast, the character of my design.

§ 3. To analyze the meaning of words into verbal and unverbal, is, I suppose, new, and it is as useless as new, unless I am correct in the above assumption; that words are unmeaning sounds when they possess no ultimate signification that is unverbal. As this character of words pervades all I shall say, I bring it prominently into consideration at the commencement of our discussions, that if the assumption is fallacious, the fallacy may be readily and speedily detected. Words have, heretofore, been defined as signs of ideas, and the meaning of words has been sought in the ideas of which the words are said to be the signs; but ideas are often composed partially or wholly of words; hence, to deem words signs of ideas, will make words signs of other words, while I desire to contemplate words with reference only to their unverbal meaning. My design will, therefore, be best foreshadowed by saying that I shall deem words as signs of only unverbal things.

§ 4. But what are unverbal things? The term seems to convey no definite meaning when I occasionally use it in conversation. Indeed, after much effort, I am not always successful in making my hearers understand the difference that exists between words and unverbal things. We can eat unverbal things without thinking of their names, and we can drink, see, smell, and handle them; but to talk about them, so as to discriminate what is unverbal in the meaning of our words from what is verbal, is a difficulty which can be vanquished by only a strong effort of the intellect. Still it must be vanquished, for all I have to say relates to unverbal things, not to words; and if the discrimination between them be not fully seen, I shall be wholly unintelligible. The muster-roll of an army consists of words which name the unverbal components of the army, and when the names are called during a muster, each of the unverbal components answers to his name; could we, in the same way, call over all words and sentences of the English language, and each unverbal thing could present itself, as the word or sentence that refers to it is called, the muster would exhibit the unverbal things separated from the words that refer to them.

Unverbal things are divisible into three classes—sensible, intellectual, and moral.

§ 1. But all unverbal things cannot be sensibly thus mustered, only a portion of them being cognizable by our senses. This portion I shall classify by itself, and call them sensations—sensible things, and sometimes physical things. Physical, wherever used by me, will be as a synonym of sensible; and both terms will severally be employed to denote what any one or more of my senses can reveal to me as a sight, sound, taste, feel or smell. By saying, therefore, of any thing that it is sensible or physical, I shall only mean that it is something cognizable by some one or more of my senses. To an uneducated deaf mute sensible things must appear in entire separation from words. He sees in the heavens neither sun, moon, stars, clouds, nor firmament, but he sees the unverbal things which the words name; and he sees on the earth, neither trees, grass, men, women, houses, streets, nor water, but he sees the unverbal things that those names designate. All sensible things possess thus an unverbal existence, and all that I require at present, is to discriminate what is unverbal from what is verbal.

§ 2. Another portion of unverbal things, but not cognizable by my senses, I shall class by themselves, under the name of emotions, or internal feelings; though I may occasionally call them by other names. I refer to our appetites, desires, passions, etc. They are as discriminable from the words that name them as sensible things. A deaf mute knows them not as anger, love, vanity, hatred, jealousy, emulation, hope, fear, desire, aversion, etc., but as emotional feelings apart from any verbal designation; and they can appear the like to us, to the extent at least of enabling us to discriminate what is verbal in relation to them from what is unverbal; though we are so accustomed, from the earliest infancy, to contemplate unverbal things through the medium of words, that to contemplate anger unverbally, is at first an unintelligible requirement.

§ 3. A third class of unverbal things I shall designate as intellectual. Every known thing is intellectual that is not comprehended by one of the above two classes. By this comprehensive rule, we never need suffer any hesitation as to whether any word names an intellection or not. If the meaning of the word is not something that can be perceived unverbally by some one or more of our senses, the unverbal meaning is intellectual, unless it be emotional, as stated in the preceding section. Our senses, therefore, are a sort of Ithuriel's spear, which will at once inform us whether the signification of any word is physical or not. If its signification is neither emotional nor can be recognized unverbally by some one or more of the senses, the signification is intellectual. Take, for instance, the word physical, if I employ it without any reference to some thing that some one of my senses can perceive unverbally—the only meaning of the word will be intellectual. I labour this point unnecessarily perhaps, but it is essential to a proper understanding of the use which I shall constantly make of the words physical and intellectual.

But I have not yet shown what intellectual things are unverbally—the unverbal things which I have thus far referred to, being either sensible or emotional. I will, therefore, proceed to adduce some examples which may indicate what I mean by the unverbal meaning of intellectual things. The words memory, thought, reflection, etc., are names of some of the unverbal things of the intellect, and they can be easily recognized unverbally. When Hamlet says, he sees his father "in his mind's eye," his words refer to an intellectual conception that is entirely distinct and separable from the words which he utters. We can see the moon, also, unverbally, in our mind's eye, and the moon thus seen intellectually is easily discriminable from the word moon, or from the sensibly perceived moon. But all intellections are not, so easily as the above, discriminable from words; for instance, the conception that the sun "required a creator before it could exist." Have these intellectually conceived words any unverbal meaning—any meaning that can be discriminated from the conceived *words and from all words?* That a ship needed a creator is not an intellectual conception so much as it is a sensible experience; and to our sensible experience about ships and analogous things, the words may be said to refer when I assert that a ship needs a creator before it can exist. But when a creator is predicated by the intellect of the sun, the conceived words refer to no sensible experience with suns or with anything analogous thereto. At one period of my life, I believed that words thus conceived by the intellect, of the sun, are totally insignificant unverbally, except as they refer to our sensible experience with ships and other analogous creations of man. As a corollary from this be lief, I supposed that an uneducated deaf mute, who knows no kind of language, can possess no intellectual conceptions in relation to the sun's requiring a creator. I supposed such a mute to be as dumb intellectually as he is verbally, and to be dumb intellectually because he is dumb verbally; and accordingly that his intellect cannot conceive that the sun required a creator, till he be taught some gesticulations with his hands or fingers, analogous to the movements which we make with our organs of speech, and which we call words. I found, however, that a deaf mute manifests, by his conduct, a knowledge of some intellectual conceptions that are as seemingly verbal only as the conception of a creator in relation to the sun; for instance, he will prefer the whole of any desirable thing rather than a part, though he cannot know verbally "that the whole is greater than a part;" and he will as readily receive a single five dollar bank note as receive five notes of a dollar each, though he cannot know verbally "that things equal to the same are equal to each other." He cannot conceive verbally the relation between master and servant, master and slave; yet he can act suitably to the relations as master, servant, or slave.

In reflecting on these anomalies, and knowing that men

in all ages of the world, and in all places, have, without any possible conventionality, conceived intellectually that the sun required a creator before it could exist, I saw that the universality of the conception must proceed from the organism of the intellect; and hence, that all such conceptions, how diversified soever in verbal creed, possess an unverbal meaning in an organic impulse from which the verbal conceptions all proceed, and to which they owe their ultimate cogency. In truth, the meaning of such words is *subjective,* not *objective.* A deaf mute, therefore, though his intellect cannot conceive in words, as ours can, that the sun required a maker, will possess the intellectual organism from which the words proceed in us; and his knowledge in the premises, excluding what is taught in the Scriptures, will be equal to ours, except that he cannot apply thereto words.

So when an uneducated deaf mute is under the influence of anger, he cannot utter the verbal execrations and imprecations which anger induces us to utter, but he can feel unverbally what we feel. The verbal execrations and imprecations are merely the effects of an organic unverbal feeling, just as the verbal dogmas in relation to a creator of the sun, are merely the effects of an organic unverbal intellectual impulse; and while the said feeling and the said impulse are probably much the same in all men, the verbal execrations and imprecations that result from the feeling of anger, and the verbal dogmas that result from the intellectual impulse, will be rude and gross among an uncultivated people, and will at all times be Dutch, French, Indian, etc., according to the nationality of the speaker; and may be inarticulate screeches in a deaf mute, or gibberish in an idiot, or spasmodic screams in an infant.

As I am endeavouring to manifest a very important, and, I suppose, unrecognized unverbal meaning of intellectually conceived words, I will give another illustration of my discrimination of the unverbal meaning from the verbal. In an uneducated deaf mute the organs of speech are situated, in relation to words, somewhat like the hands of a man are situated in relation to manipulations when the man is handcuffed. His hands, though unable to perform their proper organic movements, will possess the tendency to perform them when an occasion occurs that naturally excites the movements, and the tendency may manifest itself, as we see it in infants, in some imperfect struggles; so I suppose the intellect of an uneducated mute manifests, in some guttural sounds, a tendency to conceive words on the occasions where words are organically conceived by persons who are not mutes. I have never been in a position to observe mutes, and, therefore, speak from only conjecture; but whether they thus manifest the organic tendency or not is immaterial to my purpose, which is only to discriminate intellectually conceived words from the organic unverbal impulse from which the conceived words proceed; and to show that intellectually conceived words possess an unverbal meaning in the organism of the intellect, just as verbal execrations and imprecations possess an unverbal meaning in our moral organism. In both cases the part which is principal is unverbal, while the verbal part is subordinate. The verbal part may be Chinese, Indian, Dutch, etc., without impairing the cogency of the unverbal part; and probably the verbal part may be guttural, solecistic, and incoherent, without impairing to the speaker the cogency of the unverbal part. Some men are so stupid that the verbal conceptions of their intellect are as unintelligible to hearers as an unknown tongue; still the utterance seems to satisfy the intellects of the speakers; and how far intellections, even thus manifested, differ unverbally from intellections that are manifested in better words by better cultivated men, may be problematical. We never estimate thus the intellectual condition of stupid or illiterate men, though we are accustomed to interpret somewhat thus in such men, and in all others, words that proceed from our internal feelings. The words rogue, rascal, etc., we deem epithets of endearment when we know they proceed from feelings of affection. Indeed, the feeling of love, when it is extreme, finds often in its struggles for utterance no words so expressive of its energy as those which literally are opprobrious. We know, also, that in expressing his intellectual conceptions, every man occasionally utters, inadvertently, words of an opposite conventional meaning from what he intends; still the mistaken words satisfy the organism of his intellect, as well as a correct utterance. When, too, we listen to persons who are speaking in some foreign language that is unknown to us, and reflect that such languages are numerous to the extent of several thousand, and all of them equally satisfactory to the intellects of the speakers, we may well infer that the ultimate significance of the utterances is not dependent on the sounds that are uttered, but on the intellectual organism from which the sounds proceed. This is still more evident from the translatability of every language into the words of every other language, and which manifests that the words of all languages take cognizance of like things; and what is thus like must be unverbal, for it is not verbal; and must be organic, for it is common to all men everywhere and at all periods. If this doctrine be not true, we convert into mere words all knowledge that is not sensible or emotional; that is, all knowledge that can be manifested in words only; as, for instance, all doctrinal theology, natural and revealed; words conceived by the intellect in thought or otherwise, being no more significant and no less than words uttered audibly. I shall, however, speak more on this subject hereafter. I have attempted at present to show only that all intellectual conceptions can be discriminated from words as well as sensible things and internal feelings. Intellectual conceptions are discriminable with more difficulty, because a large number of them consist of words; but an unverbal meaning underlies and is the ultimate signification of the conceived words; just as the internal feeling that dictates the execrations of anger, underlies and is the ultimate unverbal signification of the verbal execrations.

The classification of unverbal things into intellections, sensations, and emotions, assimilates to the analysis of chemistry.

§ 1. Having thus manifested what unverbal things are, and shown that they are divisible into three classes, sensible, intellectual and emotional, I mean not to characterise any one of the three classes as more or less important than any other, my design extending no further than to so analyse our knowledge that we may discriminate words from unverbal things; and the unverbal things of one of the three classes from the unverbal things of any other of the classes.

The classification which I have attempted to apply to all unverbal things assimilates to the analysis of chemistry. As chemistry shows the relation which all compounded physical things bear to a few elemental physical things that are not compounded, so I have shown the relation which words bear to things that are unverbal. And as chemistry ends its analysis when it has analysed compounds into their elements, so when I shall have analysed any given words into unverbal things my analysis will end. The elements of chemistry—hydrogen, nitrogen, oxygen, etc.—you can examine in any way you may find practicable; but you cannot change them into each other or into any physical thing more simple. They practically say to chemists as God said to Moses, "I am that I am;" that is, they alone are their own proper expositor, and unresolvable into any more elemental thing. So, after I have shown that the word memory names an intellectual thing, and you wish to know further what the said intellectual thing is unverbally, my teachings cannot answer your question except by referring you to your intellect, which alone can present the intellection to you unverbally; and when it is thus presented, and you shall wish to question it, it can answer, like the elements of chemistry, "I am that I am;" language being at the end of its unverbal signification when its meaning is traced to the unverbal things to which it refers. What I have said of the word memory, I may repeat of every other word which signifies an intellection, as thought, idea, etc. When you know the unverbal thing, impulse, or zest, to which the words refer, you know the word's unverbal meaning; and I have accomplished in relation to it all that my analysis contemplates.

§ 2. And what I have thus said of words which signify intellections, may be repeated of words which signify internal feelings, as love, hate, hope, fear, kindness, jealousy, etc. Each of the words, when used with reference to any internal feeling, means unverbally the feeling to which it refers; and when your consciousness recognizes the feeling unverbally, the feeling becomes its own best expositor; and language in relation thereto has performed its office. The like may be said of words which signify sensible things; as, for instance, the word elephant. What your senses perceive when an elephant is exhibited to you, constitutes to you the unverbal sensible meaning of the word elephant; and the like may be said of every other word whose unverbal signification is sensible.

The unverbal things of any one class are untransmutable into the unverbal things of any other class.

§ 1. But vain will be the foregoing classific discrimination between intellectual conceptions, sensible perceptions, and internal feelings, if the three classes of unverbal things differ only in the source through which they become known to me. I assume, however, much more, namely, that the unverbal things of each class are essentially different, and are inconvertible into each other; and I am anxious that these tenets shall be perceived clearly, because, if I am incorrect in them, my entire classific superstructure is fallacious and worthless. We may well suspect that our Creator is too skilful to create more than one set of organs to perform one office; but, irrespective of this assumption, and relying wholly on what we may discover experimentally and consciously, I postulate that our sensible organs, our intellectual organism, and our internal feelings, yield respectively knowledge that is different, each of the three sets yielding us knowledge that is sui generis. The senses, for instance, reveal to us that matter is divisible, but after the sensible division proceeds to a certain extent, we find that further sensible division is impossible; the intellect, however, can and will continue the division *verbally*, and finds that matter is divisible ad infinitum; and so certain is the divisional process that it is capable of mathematical demonstration. Now I insist, that when the division ceases from being sensible, it becomes only intellectual. The two "divisions" are verbally homogeneous, but they are unverbally different; one being a sensible *perception* and the other an intellectual *conception*. But you may ask me what the difference is, and I answer that it is *unverbal;* hence I cannot tell you the difference in *words*. Our knowledge is at the end of its analysis when it is traced to the unverbal things of which it is composed. The intellectual division, like the oxygen of chemistry, is unverbally what it is. It is its own best expositor, and sole revealer. So the sensible division is unverbally what it is, and its own proper expositor and sole revealer, and no words in relation thereto can aid us in discovering how it differs unverbally from an intellectual division; the mute revelations of our intellect and our senses alone can discover the difference.

§ 2. The generic and inconvertible difference which thus exists *unverbally* in things that are *verbally* homogeneous, I claim as an important discovery; and to manifest this discovery, I have been endeavouring so long and laboriously to discriminate words from their unverbal signification; and the unverbal things of the senses from the unverbal things of the intellect, etc.; for when we speak of them, we are constantly liable to disregard their unverbal differences; by reason that the same word will often signify the unverbal things of two or of all the different three classes, as we have evinced in the word division. I can, for instance, *see* that the sun shines, and I can *see* that the three angles of a triangle are equal to two right angles; but in the first case, the word "see" signifies a physical perception—a sight; and in the second case it signifies a conception of the intellect—an intellection. Again, take the word good: Thomas is good, an apple is good, an argument is good; meaning, unverbally, some benevolent internal feeling which influences Thomas, some desirable physical property possessed by the apple, and some intellectual acuteness contained in the argument. You thus perceive that we possess three classes of unverbal things, and language refers to them all indiscriminately; consequently the unverbal things of each class being as essentially different as the Dromios of Shakspeare, nothing is more important to an unsophistical appreciation of verbal learning and verbal speculations generally, than to understand the threefold unverbal character of nearly every word; and to be able to untwist into its respective unverbal strands the three-stranded cord which nearly every word may be called. Nor is the process difficult. When language speaks of anything that our senses cannot perceive *unverbally*, language is speaking of an intellection, how much soever the words may imply that the thing is physical; and when language speaks of any internal feeling that our consciousness cannot recognize *unverbally*, language is again speaking of an intellection, how much soever the words may imply an internal feeling. Nothing, therefore, can be more discriminable from each other than the unverbal things of the three classes.

§ 3. But I must not precipitate what I have to say in relation to the nature of words. I shall speak of words presently. I desire to show now only the inconvertible difference which I claim for the perceptions of the senses, the conceptions of the intellect, and for our internal feelings. I might, perhaps, safely leave the inconvertible difference as self-evident; but Providence, by making some men blind and some deaf, enables us to learn experimentally the inability of the intellect, and the inability of words, to communicate to us the unverbal information which we receive through those senses; and by a due contemplation of such and kindred cases, we shall more readily discover the inconvertibility into each other which I claim for the three classes of unverbal things, namely, sensible perceptions, intellectual conceptions, and internal feelings. If any person is already satisfied in relation to their inconvertibility into each other, he need not read what intervenes between this and the next succeeding lecture; but if he needs more light on the subject, the following considerations may yield it:—

§ 4. Truth possesses often two aspects, one so gross that every person sees it, and the other so subtile that the acute pass it unnoticed. For instance, that a blind man's intellect cannot reveal colours to him through the agency of words, or through any other agency, is obvious; while the kindred fact that no sight can be known to you which you have not seen, has been denied by even the sagacious Hume. He says, "Suppose a man is acquainted with every colour except a particular shade of blue, and then let all the shades of blue, except the above, be placed before him in an order descending gradually from the deepest blue to the lightest; and he will be able, by his imagination, to acquire a knowledge of the absent shade." But Hume is wrong. The absent shade is a sight, and nothing can reveal it unverbally to the man but his eyes.

If we cannot thus learn a new appearance, can we not by some mental elaboration commix known sights and discover the effects? No; a change of appearance is a new sight, and irremediably unknown till disclosed by our eyes. When a milliner wishes to know how a ribbon which lies before her will appear on a hat, she trusts not to her intellect to compound the two known appearances; but from a practical acquaintance with the limitation of her faculties, applies the ribbon to the hat. So, from the known inadequacy of words to reveal new sights, we employ pictures. But a person who never saw the original, will receive from its representative no sight except that of the painting. Let a youth study geography, and be competent to designate on a map or globe every kingdom, and to tell its latitude, climate, soil, productions, and appearance; his knowledge is precisely what he displays; various appearances on maps, globes, and pictures, together with words and phrases which he has learnt to associate with them. If he thinks he knows unverbally any sight which he never experienced, a visit to the countries he has been taught to speak of will undeceive him. He may recognize names of places, names of customs, and names of natural productions; but the sights will be new. All the ingenuity of man, assisted by painting, sculpture, and eloquence, cannot teach the brightest understanding the exact unverbal appearance of a pin, except by presenting to his eyes what will produce a sight that in every respect is a pin.

On the organic limitation of our visual perceptions, to which we are thus adverting, arises the efficacy of disguises. They merely introduce a new ingredient in some known appearance, as, for instance, a black wig in place of light hair. The change of appearance produced in a man by death is often only an alteration of colours; though the change renders difficult, in many cases, an identification of the body by former familiar acquaintances. The variety which seems endless in the human countenance, is the effect of a different grouping, rather than any different formation of the features and hues that unite in the countenance. The toy called the Chinese puzzle, also the kaleidoscope, operate on the above organic principle; and, with changes in the juxtaposition of a few pieces of wood or coloured glass, produce an almost endless variety of different sights, the knowledge of any one of which we shall seek in vain from the intellect, assisted by looking, no matter how long, at the pieces separately. When we see an Indian with a daub of red paint on his cheek, and when we read in the Scriptures that women were accustomed to tinge their eyes, as modern women formerly placed small black patches on their faces, we laugh at the custom, and ask what beauty can be found in a daub of red paint or a piece of black court-plaster. The beauty consists not in these, but in the change produced in the whole countenance by the new addition, and which change no intellect can anticipate. It is often great, though the effect may not accord with our present tastes.

§ 5. That the intellect can reveal to me no sight that seeing has not informed me of, is a physical truth which experience will substantiate, and I advert to it rather than press it by argument. But a kindred position is equally true of our other senses. Let an epicure prescribe some unusual mixture of known ingredients, and after his imagination has feasted on the compound, let him present it to his taste, and he will discover the inefficiency of his intellectual foreknowledge. No brilliancy of imagination nor acuteness of the intellect can perform the office of any of our senses.

§ 6. The like may be said of feelings. A person who has never felt pain (if we can conceive such a being), will possess no correct unverbal meaning of the word; and he who has felt no greater pain than a tooth-ache, may be told of the superior agonies of the gout, but he will not be able to divine the feeling. Language can refer us to any sensible knowledge we possess, but it can *reveal* to us none in its unverbal aspect that we possess not.

§ 7. We may say the same of sounds. If I have never heard a cataract, you may inform me what the sound is like; and if I have heard a similar sound, I shall be instructed; but the intellect can effect no more than such an approximation. Should you wish to acquaint a child with the sound of a cataract, his unverbal conception of it will be very erroneous; not because his intellect is less acute than yours, or language less operative on him than on you; but because his sensible experience is less than yours, and language can be sensibly significant to him of his sensible experience only. If he has heard no sound more consonant, you must refer to even the lowing of an ox. You may qualify the comparison, by saying the cataract is awfully louder; but if he has heard nothing louder, the qualification will not add to his sensible instruction, except that it may teach him intellectually, that he is still ignorant of the correct sound of a cataract.

But cannot the letters of the alphabet be combined, so that by looking at the combination, my intellect can teach me a sound that hearing has never informed me of? I may combine letters so as to denote a new sound; but the sound, so far as it is new, will be unknown to me, till my organs of speech have uttered the combination, and thus made my hearing acquainted with it. Seeing the letters can teach us a new sound, no more than it can teach sound to a deaf mute. Nor let any person suppose that his intellect can compound known sounds, and thus acquire a sound which he never heard. The most practised musician can, no more than the most unskilful, know unverbally the sound which will be produced by a new combination of familiar notes. So far as the combination will produce a sound that he never heard, so far the effect of the combination must be sensibly unknown to him, despite all the efforts of his intellect. The power of written characters, to communicate sounds to me, is limited to sounds already known by me. We accordingly find when an Englishman attempts to learn the French language by means of written directions as to the pronunciation, he will still utter only English sounds; though to a Frenchman the written directions may represent French sounds. The obstacle to the mere Englishman is *organic,* and insurmountable by any visible or intellectual contrivance whatever.

§ 8. From the inadequacy of language to teach us unverbal things not already known, arises the inefficacy of verbal instruction. A writing master may direct a child how to make a perpendicular mark; but in every particular in which the directions refer to some motion which the pupil has never produced, or to some muscular effort that he has never made, the directions are as impotent as a discourse on colours is to the blind.

Nearly every word that possesses an unverbal meaning, possesses a verbal meaning also.

§ 1. That the sensible significancy of a man's language is limited to his sensible experience would be readily admitted, were we not embarrassed with one difficulty. Bonfire names a sight, and melody a sound. If these words possessed no other signification, we should immediately understand that the unverbal import of bonfire must ever be unknown to the blind, and the unverbal import of melody unknown to the deaf. But these words, and nearly all others, name words also; and till you understand this, you will not understand clearly that our senses alone can reveal to us the sensible signification of any word. When Locke says that the meaning of rainbow can be revealed to a person who never saw one, provided he has seen red, violet, green, etc., Locke is alluding to the verbal meaning of rainbow. This meaning can be known to the blind; and I once saw a company surprised when a blind youth was exhibiting what was esteemed a triumph of education over natural defects, by giving in words a description of the appearance of rainbows. The company knew not that rainbow possesses two significations; one unverbal, which nothing can reveal but seeing, and the other verbal, that can be learnt by hearing. You may suppose that we differ from the blind; and that a verbal enumeration of the colours of a rainbow, and of their figure, size, position and arrangement, to us who know the sights which the words signify unverbally, would reveal to us a rainbow, not verbally merely, but visibly. Take, however, any one of the colours, say red: it names unverbally not one sight only, but numerous sights. Fire is red, blood is red, my hand is red, bricks are red, and an Indian is red; which of these unverbal sights is he to imagine, when you speak of the red of a rainbow?

The same remark will apply to the other colours, and to their figure, position and arrangement. But admit that a person who has never seen a rainbow, shall still have seen all its colours. Admit further, that when you enumerate the colours, he shall guess the precise red, orange, yellow, etc., to which you refer; yet, for the person to know how the colours will look *unverbally* when they are combined, will be impossible; much less, how they will appear unverbally when drawn into the shape, size and position of a rainbow. If he has seen such a combination, he has seen a rainbow; but if he has not seen the combination, language is inadequate to reveal it. After the most copious definition, and the most familiar acquaintance with the sights separately that are referred to by the defining words, a person will be conscious of a new sight the moment he sees a rainbow.

§ 2. Words also which refer to intellections and to internal feelings, possess a verbal meaning in addition to the unverbal. The instructors of the deaf may find this discrimination important. If they wish to teach a deaf mute the signification of the word joy, they should teach him its verbal signification and its unverbal. The verbal is easily taught, but the unverbal can be disclosed by only making the mute apprehend, by any method you can, the feeling within him which joy names. To understand this analytical discrimination in the meaning of words will make the mute's knowledge definite, and facilitate his acquisitions.

§ 3. I have thus, I hope, shown that our knowledge is not a cyclopedia of mere words, but that unverbal things underlie words and constitute an unverbal meaning to which words refer for all the unverbal signification the words possess. I have shown, also, that unverbal things are not homogeneous when examined unverbally, though our knowledge seems to be homogeneous when it is deemed a cyclopedia of mere words. Unverbal things are not transmutable into one another except verbally—they are revealed to us by our senses, our intellect and our internal feelings—and each of these three sets of organs furnishes us with unverbal items that are inconvertibly different from the items furnished by either or both of the other of the said three sets of organs. I will hereafter deem these doctrines as established truths, and deem every item of our unverbal knowledge either sensible, intellectual or emotional. The utility of the discrimination of our knowledge into verbal and unverbal, and of unverbal things into three heterogeneous classes, I will now endeavour to establish.

PART I.

OF THE STRUCTURE OF LANGUAGE.

LECTURE II.

THE HETEROGENEITY OF UNVERBAL THINGS DISCRIMINATED FROM THE HOMOGENEITY WITH WHICH THEY ARE FALLACIOUSLY INVESTED BY WORDS.

CONTENTS.

1. We possess but one set of words with which to speak of three inconvertibly different classes of unverbal things.
2. The verbal homogeneity must be discriminated from the unverbal diversity, or much speculative error ensues.
3. We mistake the homogeneity of words for a homogeneity of unverbal things.

§ 1. We have seen, by the preceding introductory lecture, that while we contemplate our knowledge through the medium of words, we cannot discriminate what is intellectual from what is sensible, etc. We adduced an example of this indiscrimination in the divisibility of matter; the sensible divisibility and the intellectual divisibility being verbally homogeneous, though as heterogeneous unverbally as oxygen and hydrogen. While we deem homogeneous the sensible divisibility and the intellectual, we are as much astonished at the logical divisibility ad infinitum of matter, as we are at a feat of unsuspected jugglery; but when we discover that the divisibility is generically different in the two cases, our astonishment is as much relieved as when we find that the handkerchief which the juggler cut into pieces, is not the handkerchief which he subsequently restores to us uncut.

The above is only an example of the fallacious homogeneity which our knowledge assumes continually when contemplated through the medium of words; and we shall find, as we proceed in our discussions, that to discriminate the generic differences that pertain to unverbal things, and which the structure of language leads us to disregard, will relieve our speculative knowledge and our logic from sophistry, mystery and perplexity; and that the want of such discrimination constitutes the least suspected, but the greatest, most general, and most surprising error of the age. If any person will refer to the word "matter" in Rees's New Cyclopedia, he will find a summary of what the most eminent men of different periods have said of matter, and he will be painfully conscious of the fog which surrounds the subject by their deeming intellectual conceptions homogeneous with sensible things. Acuteness of intellect, in labours thus misdirected, but darkens more elaborately what it strives to elucidate. The indiscrimination between what is sensible and what is intellectual constitutes the radical defect of all metaphysics and all logic, and in view of the wreck of intellectual effort the indiscrimination has occasioned, countless volumes that have descended to us through the course of ages, and to which we are still adding, are like the blood on the hands of

Macbeth, "a sorry sight!" Indeed, till a man learns to discriminate the generic difference between things sensible, intellectual and emotional; till he learns to regard their verbal homogeneity as only a quality of language; his knowledge, when contemplated through the medium of words, will be as fallacious as a child's who shall not discriminate the generic difference between the events of the "Arabian Nights," and the events of history—a difference that consists in only that one set of events are intellectual conceptions; and the other set, sensible performances. But the principle is too complex to be discussed thus in gross, and I will proceed to manifest it in several of its various phases, but commencing with the most simple examples.

Perhaps nothing are deemed more unsuspectedly homogeneous than our thoughts, and to their verbal homogeneity pertains much of the mysteriousness connected with them. A little reflection will, however, enable us to discover that thoughts, instead of being homogeneous, can be classified into six strongly-marked unverbal, generic diversities. Professor Stewart says, "Some men, in even their private speculations, not only use words as an instrument of thought, but form the words into sentences." What is thus alleged is true of all men; but the remark attaches to only one kind of thoughts. When we pronounce million *inaudibly,* it is a thought; when we pronounce it *audibly,* it is a word. The like may be said of every word. We can better see that verbal thoughts are only inaudible words, when we reflect that every oral word consists *un-*

verbally of a sound and certain movements of the breath, lips, tongue, and other vocal organs. This analysis dispels part of the mystery of verbal thoughts, for we usually deem a word nothing but sound; and are conscious that our verbal thoughts are not *sounds*.

Verbal thoughts are, unverbally, a movement of some of the vocal organs, and occasionally of the breath. If, for instance, you repeat in thought the alphabet, you will occasionally detect a slight agency of some of the vocal organs, especially of the tongue. The more freely we permit the tongue's movements, the more distinctly we can think the alphabet. If you stand before a mirror and protrude your tongue, you will often see it either dilate or thicken, as each letter is pronounced in thought. The experiment must be made with letters whose articulation is lingual. And again, we cannot think the word George while we are speaking the word Thomas; nor can we pronounce the word Thomas, while we are thinking George. Utterance is limited also to successive syllables, and verbal thoughts are similarly limited to successive syllables. The phrase "Our father," we can no more condense into one thought, than we can pronounce the words in one articulation; hence, though verbal thoughts and oral words are not identities in name, the similarity between them is close. A deaf mute is as deficient of verbal thoughts as he is of oral words; nor can an infant possess verbal thoughts till he has learned to speak. A Frenchman thinks French words, and an Englishman English. An uneducated man thinks ungrammatical sentences, and a rude man, vulgar sentences. Professor Blair says truly, that a person who is learning to arrange his words correctly, is learning to think correctly.

§ 2. But the Professor's remark is applicable to only verbal thoughts, and to them I alluded in my introductory lecture when I said, "that ideas are often composed partially or wholly of words." When the intellect conceives verbal thoughts in explanation of oral words, we call the explanatory thoughts an idea; but they are only the substitution of one set of words for another. Such substitution constitutes an artificial circle which we may travel around interminably without advancing a step in unverbal knowledge; though we may suppose we are piling Ossa on Pelion, erecting a new Babel, and peering therefrom into the highest heavens that our intellect conceives to exist. Peer thus we may, I admit, but such peerings signify, unverbally, the subjective conceptions of the intellect, not what the words mean unverbally when they refer to sensible things. Of such verbal conceptions I shall speak in another place, and will not further anticipate the topic here.

§ 3. But verbal thoughts are only one kind of the six generic varieties into which thoughts are divisible. We can think the appearance of the moon, and the appearance is a visual thought. Visual thoughts possess the evanescence of vision. They appear and vanish. They possess also the comprehensiveness of vision. We comprehend in

3

one gaze the starry firmament, and our visual thought of the firmament is as capacious as the gaze, and apparently as remote from our contact. We may, in some instances, detect a slight agency of the eyes in the production of visual thoughts. We keep the eyes fixed, and, in a manner, direct our attention to the eyes when we want to recall in visual thought some absent sight. The actor who, in personating Hamlet, says, "My father! I think I see him now," will instinctively stare.

The remaining four kinds of thoughts are characteristically sounds, tastes, feels, and smells. When I recall in thought the last pressure of my hand by an absent friend, the pressure rests seemingly upon my hand, with the contaction which pertains to the sense of feeling, though peculiarly modified. Smells, when recalled in thought, possess the limitation that pertains to the perception of odours; for we can no more combine in one unverbal thought, the distinct fragrance of a rose, and the fetor of assafœtida, than we can realize the odours separately in one inspiration. We also snuff up the air when we endeavour to recall unverbally some absent odour. To recall sounds in thought conforms so nearly to actual hearing, that I have heard a musician require silence from his auditors when he was recollecting a tune. Many voices uttered confusedly together, can be recalled in thought in one clamour, as we heard them; and in this, the thinking of sounds differs characteristically from the thinking of words: they can be thought of in only the syllabick succession of oral utterance. Tastes, when recalled in thought, possess the singleness which attends the perceptions of tastes. Vinegar and water, for instance, when placed together in the mouth, combine to form a single taste, and thought cannot present us, unverbally, the two tastes simultaneously. Some acids will produce a flow of saliva, and to think unverbally of the acids will often produce a like flow. In speaking also of absent luxuries of the palate, we often say, the recalled tastes make us "smack our lips," etc. Our forms of speech exhibit our organization about as necessarily and as accurately as wax exhibits the lineaments of the seal which impresses it; and a better philosophy floats in our colloquial phraseology than phraseology receives credit for.

§ 4. Whether madness uniformly affects alike all of the six kinds of a maniac's thoughts, may be worth the examination of physicians. When the late Attorney-General of the United States, Mr. Legare, was suffering under his last illness, he called for water, but on its presentation to him, he rejected it, saying the tumbler was full of ants. His attendants assured him that the glass and water were pure, and that the apparent ants were a delusion of his sight. He then drank the water. This supremacy of his intellect over his visual perceptions, discriminates such a delusion as his from intellectual insanity. How many of the senses may concur in any delusion, and the intellect retain its supremacy over the deranged senses, may be deserving of note, when such cases can be observed. A lady has been long an inmate of the Utica Lunatic Asylum, who continually hears audible words which her intellect deems the conversation of invisible people, she refusing to believe that the words are simply a derangement of her hearing, and hence she is properly accounted intellectually insane. A paralysis of the organs of speech affects verbal thoughts nearly as much as it affects oral words; while the other five kinds of thought are unimpaired. The paralytic, in a case like the above, recognizes by sight his friends, but he cannot recollect their names; he recalls in visual thought his absent friends, with a like inability of recollecting their names.

Every person's memory is perhaps better in some one of the six classes of thoughts than in the others. I can recollect sights better than words. Musicians may recollect sounds better than words or sights. The recollection of words is the only branch of memory we usually cultivate at schools, and this limitation may be a defect in our instruction. Practically, we are well aware of the generic diversity which exists in our thoughts as above classified into six varieties. I heard a gentleman refuse to look on his deceased friend, because he wished to think of his friend in no other way than as he appeared when alive. The remark surprised no one. With verbal thoughts, he can think of the deceased in any state of decay that language can express, whether he view him or not; but with visual thoughts, he can think of only the sights he can recall. I shall say no more of thoughts. I have introduced them as only subsidiary to my present topic, the verbal homogeneity of things that unverbally are heterogeneous.

§ 5. The fallacious homogeneity assumed by unverbal things when contemplated verbally, first presented itself to me in a physiological examination to which I, many years ago, subjected our senses. One of my theorems affirmed, that "what seeing cannot inform me of is not sight." When, for instance, an infant is situated in a dark room, and the room becomes suddenly illuminated by the introduction therein of a lighted candle, the sensible appearances alone will not teach the infant that the candle and the illumination are connected as cause and effect; and what is thus true of an infant is equally true of a man who shall be as inexperienced as an infant. The causal connection, therefore, which in such a case exists between the illumination and the candle, is not a sight, or seeing could inform the infant thereof. Seeing sees only the sequence of the two sensible events, the introduction of the candle and the illumination of the room; and after a thousand experiments of the same kind, seeing will still see only the sequence of the two sensible events. But we learn eventually that the candle and the illumination of the room are causally connected, and if the knowledge is not sight, the knowledge must proceed from some other inlet than the senses; hence gradually arose in me the conception, (common enough, no doubt, in many men,) that our causal knowledge is intellectual. But with this common conception arose the further conception, and of which in part the present lecture is a consequence, that language yields us no intimation that a causal connection, as conceived by the intellect, is different generically from a sensible connection, as perceived by the senses in the links which compose an iron chain. While the unverbal generic difference is not recognized between the two verbally homogeneous connections, nothing but confusion must ensue from any verbal speculations, like those which Hume rendered famous, in relation to the connection which exists between cause and effect. The connection of cause and effect is therefore only a conception of the intellect; while the connection of two links of a chain is a perception of the senses.

Night follows day sensibly, and day follows night; and after Hume had defined cause and effect to be nothing but invariable sensible succession, the question has been often asked, sportively I suppose, whether night is the cause of day, or day the cause of night. The question, however intended, is useful, for if the words cause and effect possess a sensible meaning only, (an invariable sequence of two given sensible events,) night is the cause of day, or day the cause of night. But the intellect sees not in night and day the relation of cause and effect, hence neither is deemed the cause of the other. When, however, the sun arises and daylight succeeds the sun's emergence, our senses inform us of only the two sensible events; but in addition to these, and wholly different therefrom, our intellect informs us that the sun is the cause of the light.

Lawyers, whose profession is employed about unverbal

differences rather than verbal homogeneities, are well versed in the distinction which exists between sensible perceptions and intellectual conclusions. If I see William stab Peter, and see Peter fall down and die immediately thereafter, seeing perceives only the sensible facts; but whether the fall of Peter and his death were effects of the stab, are intellectual conclusions which may be decided better by a surgeon of practical experience who was not present at the stabbing, than by an unprofessional and inexperienced man who saw it. If a witness, misled by the homogeneity of language, were to testify that he saw William murder Peter, he would be forthwith told to testify to what he saw, and that the intellect of the jury would determine whether Peter was murdered, and whether William was the murderer. In our day, many people will testify that they have seen tables gyrated, and heard tables rapped, by the spirits of the dead. Such people are unaware of the generic difference between what is sensible in such testimony, and what is intellectual. In all that is sensible, (the gyrations and raps,) every person will concur, such concurrence being a peculiarity of sensible perceptions, and unaffected by localities or periods of time; but when the intellect superadds a conception in words, of some modus operandi, by which the tables are gyrated and rapped, the conceived words may assume some three thousand and sixty different kinds of utterance, that being about the number of different languages which are said to exist in the world at the present day. The intellectually conceived words may differ also, not vernacularly only, as above supposed, but every man of the millions of men who now occupy the earth, may express his intellectual conceptions of the modus operandi of table rappings, etc., in words differently collocated, and in different words, according to his individual intelligence, experience, ignorance, credulity, etc. To recognize the difference which thus exists generically between what we see and hear in relation to tables, and what the intellect will conceive to be the cause thereof, may be useful in dispelling the delusion which deems homogeneous the intellectually conceived cause and the sensibly perceived movements and sounds. I could easily say more on the subject, and especially in relation to the absurdity of the popularly assigned cause, but it is not properly within the purview of my discussions. I cannot, however, refrain from adding, that such gyrations and rappings are as evincive of a physical cause, as the appearance of a house or clock; and for precisely the same reasons.

§ 6. What we have said of cause and effect may be repeated of numerous words which, like them, signify intellectual conceptions, though language fails to mark the generic distinction between them and sensible perceptions. When I see a man and a boy, I may relate the event in those words; and I may say, also, they are father and son. Verbally the two expressions are homogeneous, but unverbally the expressions refer to generic differences; the man and boy being sensible perceptions, while the relations of father and son are intellectual conceptions. The like may be said of master and apprentice, master and pupil, master and slave, etc.; all are intellectually conceived relations, not sensible appearances. So when we see a man placing one tier of bricks on another with mortar and trowel, we see nothing sensible but the man and his operations; but in addition to these, and generically different and separable therefrom, the intellect sees the relation of building and builder, construction and constructor, making and maker, design and designer. When I see one man whipping another, my senses see only the sensible actions and the sensible actors; but besides these, and wholly uncognizable by my senses, my intellect may see in the two men and their sensible conduct, the relation of executioner and criminal, oppressor and oppressed, tyrant and subject, etc.

Nothing is more mysterious to us than Time, still its superior mystery over other things arises from our unconsciousness that time is only a conception of the intellect. Our senses perceive objects successively, our internal feelings follow each other successively, our thoughts are also successive, and from all these experimental successions the intellect conceives the notion of time; but if we endeavour to estimate time as something different from an intellectual conception, especially if we deem it homogeneous with sensibly perceived objects, we of course convert time into a mystery. The like may be said of space. What is sensibly perceptible in space is no way mysterious, but what we conceive intellectually of space is very mysterious, when we deem the conception homogeneous with sensible perceptions.

We may say the like of power, quantity, quality, number, infinity, omnipotence, omnipresence, omniscience, etc. Whatever is sensibly perceptible in relation to any of them is no more mysterious than any other sensible perception; but what we conceive intellectually of any of them is very mysterious, when we deem the conception homogeneous with any thing that is sensibly perceptible.

When I look at a man vigorous in health, and, perhaps, in a moment or more thereafter look at the same man dead, my intellect, and the intellect of every man, savage and civilized, philosopher and clown, will *organically* conceive from the change, what we shall in vain seek physically, though the intellect, as in cause and effect, may express its conceptions of the change in words that are homogeneous with sensible perceptions; as, for instance, that "the vital spark is extinguished that burned so brightly a moment previously;" that "the soul which was united with the body is become disunited and fled," etc. Men often speak of these verbally expressed intellections as Hume speaks of the connection of cause and effect, and deem mysterious that we cannot *see* how the soul is united to the body; as Hume deemed mysterious that we cannot see the *connection* between cause and effect; but we cannot *see* how the soul is united to the body, and how effects are connected to causes, for the words refer in each case to a conception of the intellect, not to any thing that is sensible. The admission that the union and connection cannot be seen, proves that they are intellectual. We are organized with mental as well as sensible inlets of knowledge, and if we will give all words an interpretation that refers to sensible perceptions, (deeming homogeneous intellectual conceptions and sensible perceptions,) the resulting verbal mystery is an error of our speculations, and nothing more. Where is next week? said a child to me lately; and truly, where is next week? If we look for it *sensibly*, our inability to find it involves much mystery; but next week exists in only the intellect, and when thus considered, its mysterious undiscoverability vanishes with the delusion on which the sensible search is founded.

§ 7. We place an acorn in the ground and it becomes an oak; we eat food, and it sustains life and increases our strength; we will, and our limbs obey the impulse; we sleep, and become unconscious; we awake, and consciousness returns. In these and countless other cases, the parts which are sensible in the performances constitute only a portion of our knowledge thereof, another important part being intellectually conceived; but the intellectual part being conceived in words that express also sensible perceptions, we recognize not the generic difference which pertains to the unverbal meaning of the words in these different uses of them, and accordingly deem perplexingly mysterious that we cannot discover sensibly the parts that are only intellectually conceived. If we reflect on the words that refer to the intellectual part of our knowledge, in cases like the above, we shall find that they proceed from attempts of the intellect to assimilate its conceptions to physical operations; as, for instance, when the senses perceive, as just stated, that a man who a moment ago could walk, speak, and argue, is now dead—a mass of inert matter that will speedily decompose and corrupt—the intellect will assimilate the change to some sensible processes that the intellect conceives to be analogous; for instance, to the extinction of a candle, ("the vital spark is fled;") to the stoppage of a coach by the removal of the horses, ("the soul is departed from the body;") to the fall of an infant when the nurse withdraws its support, ("God has withdrawn His sustaining hand,") etc., etc., to the end of the many analogies that the intellect can see between life and death. I object to none of the intellectual assimilations, for they are organic, but I object to deeming the assimilations homogeneous with sensible perceptions. The assimilations possess a *subjective* meaning in our *organism,* not an *objective* meaning in *sensible things,* as they verbally seem to possess; hence no proper reason exists for surprise and mystery that we cannot see *sensibly* what, on any occasion, we conceive *intellectually.*

If you scratch ever so lightly with a pin at the end of a long piece of solid timber, the scratch will be heard by any person who places his ear at the other end of the timber. The intellect accounts for the result of this experiment by conceiving that the sound passes through the timber. The passing through the timber thus referred to, is a conception of the intellect, but it is no way discriminated verbally from a physical passage through, like the passage that would be made by the boring of an auger, or like the passage of a flow of water through a pipe. I admit that the intellect may be unable to account for the experiment with the timber, (that is, may be unable to assimilate it to tangible operations,) in any better way than by an analogy with the passage of water through a pipe; but we need not deem both "passing through" as homogeneous unverbally as they are verbally. Such a discrimination, however, we never make, but, unwisely, I think, employ the verbal equivoke, to excite surprise at the subtility of sound which thus can glide through *solid timber;* we are surprised because we mistake an intellectually conceived passage for a physical passage. So when the electric telegraph transmits a communication over a thousand miles of wire, the transmission from one end of the wire to the other is nearly instantaneous. The intellect may find no better way of assimilating to our physical operations the transmission, than by conceiving that an electric fluid *passes* or *flows* instantaneously from one end of the wire to the other; but if we deem such intellectually conceived flow and passage homogeneous with a physical flow and passage, (as, for instance, the passage of a stage-coach over a turnpike, or the passage of a cannon ball through the air,) we astonish ourselves needlessly and fallaciously by confounding intellectual conceptions with physical things.

If the conceptions of the intellect and the informations of our senses possessed no other evidences of their heterogeneity than the character of their results, as in the above examples, we might reasonably suspect that some delusion existed, though we might be unable to tell what it is; just as we know the tricks of a professed juggler to be deceptive, though we may be unable to detect the deception. But if this test be cogent in the foregoing examples, what shall we say to speculations like the following, whose mystery is resolvable in no other way than by the radical heterogeneity that exists unverbally between things intellectually conceived and things sensibly perceived. Doctor Nieuwentyt, in his Religious Philosophy, Vol. III., p. 865, thus discourses of the divisibility of the particles of matter:—He has computed intellectually, and doubtless with accuracy, that "from an inch of candle, vastly more particles of light will issue during its consumption, than a thousand times a thousand millions times the number of sands the whole earth can contain."

Or, take what is daily taught in our schools, that light travels, or moves consecutively, from the sun to the earth, with a velocity equal to about twelve millions of miles in a minute; or, as it is often stated, a million of times more swiftly than the flight of a ball fired from a cannon. I object not to the doctrine, and know it is logically satisfactory to the intellect; but when we deem the intellectually conceived consecutive velocity and motion of light, homogeneous with the sensibly perceived consecutive motion of a car along a railroad, or even of a cannon ball, we are fallaciously confounding intellectual conceptions with physical perceptions. The phraseology forms no part of my objection, whatever form the phraseology may assume; but I contend that a generic difference exists between what is intellectually conceived and what is sensibly perceived, and that a disregard of the unverbal difference is a needless verbal mystification and obfuscation of what Providence permits us to know clearly in its unverbal reality. The generic unverbal difference may be deemed unimportant, between what we conceive intellectually and what we can perceive sensibly; but if the discrimination be unimportant, why are we so anxious, as we seem to be, to identify, for example, the intellectually conceived consecutive motion of light with sensibly perceived consecutiveness. Of our proneness to such verbal equivokes, the following, which I extract from a highly valuable recent periodical publication, is only a common example in its kind, though peculiarly ingenious in its matter. It is designed to generically assimilate to physical operations the intellectually conceived consecutive speed of light, and also the intellectually conceived distance from the earth of the sun and other celestial bodies:—

"Imagine," says the writer, "a railway from here to the sun. How many miles is the sun from us? Why, if we were to send a baby in an express train, going incessantly a hundred miles an hour, without making any stoppages, the baby would grow to be a boy; the boy would grow to be a man; the man would die without seeing the sun; for it is distant more than a hundred years from us. But what is this compared to Neptune's distance?

Had Adam and Eve started by our railway to go from Neptune to the sun, at the rate of fifty miles an hour, they would not have got there yet, for Neptune is more than six thousand years from the centre of our system."

If intellections are unverbally homogeneous with sensible things, we may well wonder why verbal assimilations like the foregoing so surprise and amuse us that we employ them as piquantly as we employ ventriloquism and legerdemain. Astronomy has yielded so many practical benefits to mankind, that it can well dispense with any éclât that may proceed from our deeming its intellectual conceptions homogeneous unverbally with sensible perceptions. I may say the like of chemistry, whose similarly fallacious verbal assimilations I shall occasionally advert to; but only for the purpose of illustrating my views of language; hence if my strictures on astronomy and chemistry shall themselves be deemed unsound, as they may be from my defective knowledge of those sciences, my strictures will still be useful to the end for which alone I shall introduce them.

§ 8. Our dissatisfaction with intellectually conceived relations and agencies, till the intellect can in some way theoretically materialize them,—as, for instance, our dissatisfaction with the intellectual relation of cause and effect, till we can theoretically superadd a material or physical connection between the cause and the effect,—may be an inevitable result of our organization, or it may be simply a prejudice resulting from our sensible employments. We satisfy hunger and thirst by sensible appliances; we move by sensible operations; by sensible agencies we speak, hear, see, taste, feel, smell, propagate our species, construct ships, houses, and innumerable other things, fight battles, and employ ourselves incessantly; hence when a spark produces an explosive effect on gunpowder, and we can perceive only a sensible juxtaposition between the spark and the powder, we are dissatisfied till the intellect will conceive some rationale that will analogize or assimilate the intellectually conceived action of the spark to our personal sensible agencies in the production of effects.

So when two billiard balls rebound upon coming in contact with each other, we can perceive sensibly nothing but the contact; but in addition to all which the senses can perceive, the intellect of every beholder will conceive some impulse in the concussion, analogous to the sensible force which a man is conscious of exerting when he pushes any thing from him, or hurls a stone from his hand; and when we see a needle rush towards a magnet, the intellect will conceive some physical emanation from the magnet which *draws* the needle towards the magnet, as our hand draws sensibly to our body some object at which we are pulling; and when we stand before a fire, and feel warmth or heat, the intellect will conceive some material radiation from the fire to sensibly *connect* our body therewith, and thereby to assimilate the effect which we feel, to our mode of operating by sensible contact; and when we look at distant hills, trees, and fields, and hear distant sounds, the intellect will insist on theoretically assimilating the organic processes of seeing and hearing to our personal processes of tangible contaction; and hence will conceive that rays of light radiate physically from the distant visible object to the retina of the eye, and that appulses of air from the distant sonorous body, *strike* physically the tympanum of the ear; and when water rushes up a tube from which the air is exhausted, the intellect will insist on conceiving some material process of suction in the vacuum, analogous to the process with which we sensibly suck fluids into our mouth; or some process of material pressure on the water analogous to the sensible pressure we exert upon bodies with our hands or weight; and when we look at the sun, moon, and stars, the intellect will insist on attributing to them tangibility, solidity, and other constant physical properties that are found in the bodies which we handle; and when a physician administers medicine, his intellect will insist on conceiving some material modus operandi by which the expected result in the patient is to be produced. A man can no more prevent his intellect from conceiving such material machinery, than he can prevent his sight from seeing objects that are before it; or prevent his ears from hearing sounds; but he is not compelled to deem such conceptions homogeneous with sensible things. Such conceptions constitute the theories of scientific men, and the hypotheses of the unscientific—the theories of optics, of acoustics, of medicine, of magnetism, of combustion, of the generation of a fœtus, the cosmogony of the world, the formation of metals, the alternation of the seasons, etc.,

etc., through the whole circle of speculative knowledge; and I believe I am not mistaken in assuming that we never discriminate such conceptions of the intellect from physical things;—indeed such a discrimination would divest the conceptions of their chief charm, the fallacious homogeneity constituting a sort of fairy land in which we delight to wander.

That theories are useful, only accords with the general fact that our intellect is adapted to our physical powers, as our physical powers are adapted to the material universe. If, however, we mistake for physical, the intellectually conceived emanations from magnets, the radiations of caloric from fire, of rays of light to the eye, the aerial appulses to the ear, the pressure on water, etc., we are not discriminating the heterogeneity of unverbal things from the homogeneity of words.

So satisfied are we with the self-sufficiency of sensible agency, that the attempts of phrenologists to account for intellectual manifestations by sensible organs, is deemed a species of atheism; though our sensible organs are often as apparently perfect after death, when they are powerless, as during life, when they are powerful. In truth, therefore, our sensible powers and our intellectual are alike wonderful. They are severally just what they are, and as they are; but we superadd to their inevitable wonder, the unnecessary wonder that we cannot find, sensibly, a power, causation, impulse, vitality, etc., that are only intellectual; and that we cannot find, in intellectual operations, a machinery that is sensible; results which ought to teach us that the two classes of things are different and inconvertible, except verbally.

In the conception of theories, the intellect is not, however, restricted to physical agencies, but may employ an internal feeling as the agent, if the intellect can discover an analogy between the effect on us of such an internal feeling, and the conceived efficiency to be accounted for; "Let there be light! and there was light," can be accounted for satisfactorily to the intellect, by its deeming the *will* of *Deity* to be the efficient agent. *Horror* moves us effectively, and hence Nature's horror of a vacuum accounted formerly as satisfactorily to the intellect for the ascent of water up a vacuum, as the pressure of the atmosphere accounts for the ascent at present. So the intellect can theoretically account for the instantaneous transmission of electricity over a thousand miles of wire, by conceiving that electricity possesses the nature of thought; indeed I have heard its operations thus accounted for. Such a conception assimilates the transmission with our personal operations, and the transmission becomes immediately satisfactory.

§ 9. I have now completed three steps in my progress. I have manifested the difference that exists between words and unverbal things; I have shown, also, that unverbal things are divisible into three generically and inconvertibly different classes, sensible, intellectual, and emotional; and lastly, that the heterogeneity of unverbal things is disregarded by language, words implying a homogeneity, or at least manifesting no sign of the generic differences that exist in unverbal things. To the steps thus accomplished I wish to give some prominence before I proceed further, and, therefore, place these remarks as mile-posts, to prevent the said completed steps from escaping notice. Any reader who comprehends satisfactorily the said three accomplished steps, may proceed at once to the next succeeding lecture; the intervening remarks being chiefly valuable as a means of illustrating still further the heterogeneity which language disregards in unverbal things.

§ 10. The indiscrimination which is thus inherent in language encourages various speculative errors, as I have endeavoured to show; but we are not left without an ability to discover that the indiscrimination is not an unmitigated evil; indeed we can find that it is attended with utilities which more than compensate for its evils; and that the indiscrimination is founded in our intellectual organism, and assimilates with all other evils that proceed from our organization, in being unavoidable rather than unnecessary; for instance, sensible things we can exhibit to each other unverbally, and the unverbal meaning of words is learnt by children through the means of such exhibitions only; but intellectual conceptions we cannot exhibit to each other unverbally, hence children nor men could ever learn the meaning of words that should signify intellections only. The intellect is, therefore, compelled, if it speak of its conceptions at all to other men, to employ words that refer to sensible things. To provide for this dilemma, the intellect of every man is so organized, that it sees an analogy between its own conceptions and sensible things; so that when you tell me that an electric fluid passes over, or flows through a telegraphic wire, my intellect recognizes immediately the intellection to which the language refers. Even a deaf mute who knows no language, were he acquainted with both the flowing of water through a pipe, and the communication of written messages by means of the wires of a telegraph, would probably recognize intellectually an analogy between the two processes; and if this conjecture be correct, it evinces that the sensible flow and the intellectual conception are spoken of by the same words from an organic tendency of the intellect, not from any conventional usage. Indeed, the usage cannot be conventional, the same kind of phraseology being common to all languages and to all periods of time.

§ 11. Internal feelings manifest themselves sensibly almost as distinctly as physical objects; hence we can speak of internal feelings, love, rage, anger, etc., without employing therefor words that signify physical objects. Internal feelings contrast thus very observably with intellectual conceptions, and by reflecting on the difference between their external manifestibility we can more easily understand why we speak of intellectual conceptions with words that signify physical objects, and adopt a different course in speaking of internal feelings.

So knowable by sensible signs are our internal feelings,

that painters depict the signs on canvass, and our intellect recognizes, in brutes and in even inanimate sensible things, appearances analogous to the said sensible signs; hence in all periods of time, and in all languages, we find such expressions as *violent* winds, *furious* storms, *hateful* weather, *kind* showers, *vicious* horses, *stubborn* ropes, *frantic* torrents, *impetuous* eloquence, etc. By like external signs, deaf mutes can be taught as readily the unverbal meaning of the words rage, love, pride, etc., as the mutes can be taught the unverbal meaning of the words fire, horse, cat, etc.

But I have no concern with either intellectual concep tions or internal feelings, except to explain why internal feelings can be spoken of by peculiar words; and why the intellect is compelled to speak of its own conceptions in words whose original meaning is sensible things. I will, however, add that a great utility is discoverable in the sensible external manifestibility of our internal feelings. We are thereby able to conserve our personal safety by ascertaining the presence in brute animals and in our human associates, of rage, anger, etc., before we become injured thereby. A kindred utility attends the opposite principle of the undiscoverability by external sensible manifestations of our thoughts and other intellections. Every man's intellect is thus organically able to think and conceive with perfect occlusion, though surrounded by multitudes of inquisitive observers. The benefit which we derive from this freedom of thought is itself sufficient to compensate for the consequent evil of organically thinking and conceiving intellectually in words that ordinarily signify sensible things.

§ 12. I ought, perhaps, before I conclude the present topic, to advert to a radical difference which, besides their heterogeneity, exists between intellectual conceptions and internal feelings;—internal feelings exist in different degrees of intensity in different men, and are more excitable in some men than in others; but in the numerical variety of feelings that pertain to men, any two men are like pianos that possess the same number of keys, and consequently possess latently the same numerical variety of sounds. Intellectual conceptions are different in the above respects. A child who should hear at the end of a stick of timber, the scratch made with a pin at the other end, would not infer intellectually, that the sound passed *through* the timber, as water passes through a pipe, if he had never seen such a passage of water; the intellect conceiving theories from only the sensible facts that are known to it; hence we are constantly changing our theories as we become acquainted with new sensible facts; and hence the often noted peculiarity that chemists account for things by assimilating them to chemical processes; mechanics account for them by mechanical processes; mathematicians, by mathematical processes, etc., etc. In constructing theories the intellect obeys an organic impulse, but the form of the theory will depend, as above stated, on the accidental knowledge of the theorist. I will not anticipate what I shall say hereafter when I shall treat particularly of "the unverbal meaning of intellectually conceived words," but the unverbal meaning of all theories is *subjective*, (in the intellect, not in the objective universe;) hence the accidental verbal form which the theory on any subject assumes in different men, at different periods, may affect the practical utility of the theory, but all the theories will, *subjectively considered*, possess the same unverbal meaning.

From the foregoing account of the mode in which the intellect constructs theories, we may see why medical theories continue, after the efforts of centuries, to be but little improved. The processes of generation, the functions of vital organs, the commencement and progress of diseases, are manifestations so unique, that the intellect can see no analogy between them and any different operation; especially none between them and tangible operations, which supply our most satisfactory theoretical agencies. This is perhaps an insurmountable obstruction to the progress of medicine as a science, and compels it to be empirical. Any way, our medical practitioners theorize less than their early predecessors, without having yet been able to conceive any substitute for theories as a guide to medical practice, in advance of actual experiments. But these are speculations only incidental to a correct analysis of language; and having now exhibited, though I fear too desultorily, the heterogeneity of unverbal things, and the homogeneity with which language invests them, I will proceed to the consideration of another equally important and equally undetected characteristic of words.

LECTURE III.

UNVERBAL MULTIPLICITY DISCRIMINATED FROM ITS FALLACIOUS VERBAL ONENESS.

CONTENTS.

1. Names analysed, and their implied oneness found to be a conception of the intellect, not an objective oneness.
2. All individuality is a conception of the intellect.
3. The intellect aggregates sensible perceptions into nominal units.
4. The intellect aggregates internal feelings into nominal units.
5. The intellect aggregates its own conceptions into nominal units.
6. The intellect aggregates into nominal units, its own conceptions, associated with certain internal feelings.
7. Of nominal units, whose unverbal components belong to two or more of the senses; or whose components are otherwise heterogeneous.

Of Physical Units.

§ 1. The views of language presented in this lecture, like the views presented in the former, were suggested to me many years ago in the investigation which I made of the powers of our senses, and to which I have already alluded. I assumed that the information which any one of the senses yielded to me, cannot be yielded by the other senses singly or conjointly; still, practical results contradicted the assumed truth. Some blind men can recognize colours by the sense of touch; some have lectured and written books on visual subjects. A man not blind, can discern a globe by either seeing or feeling, and can recognize an orange by either the taste, the smell, the sight, or the feel; how then is the assertion true, that what one of my senses informs me of, no one or more of my other senses can inform me of? Two senses can inform me of the same globe, and four senses of the same orange. The dilemma perplexed me long, till, finally, I discovered that the difficulty lay in language. It applies the word orange to the sensible group (taste, smell, sight, feel,) that four of my senses severally disclose to me; hence the information which I receive from the respective four senses is one in only the name orange, that is applied in common to all the four sensible revelations.

To relieve myself from embarrassments like the foregoing, and to manifest unmistakeably in future, that what any one of my five senses informs me of, no one or more of my other senses can inform me of, I denominated as sight merely every information that I received from seeing; as feel, every information I received from the sense of feeling; as sound, every information that I received from the sense of hearing; as taste, every information I received from the sense of tasting; and as smell, every information I received from the sense of smelling. Instead, therefore, of saying that both seeing and feeling informed me of a globe, (and thereby implying that what seeing informs me of, I am informed of by feeling also,) I said, seeing informs me of the sight globe, and feeling informs me of the feel globe.

But still a difficulty arose; the globe is only one thing, while my analysis converts it into two things, a sight globe and a feel globe. If the oneness of the two globes is simply a contrivance of language, as I had supposed of the orange, all languages would not concur, as they do, in calling the sight globe and the feel globe one thing. The uniformity seemed too extensive to be conventional, hence gradually became evident to me, that the oneness of the globe, not being sensible, must be intellectual; the intellect being so *organized,* that the sight globe and the feel suggest a unit to the intellect; and language so *constituted* that it refers, in all names of things, to the intellectually conceived unit.

Besides, if the oneness were only verbal, as I had at first supposed it was, an uneducated deaf mute would not deem as one thing, the sight globe and the feel globe; but his intellect conceives the two to be a unit, as completely, no doubt, as ours. The organic tendency of the intellect to thus aggregate sensible multiplicity into intellectual units is, as I ultimately discovered, one of the essential foundations of language, names referring to these intellectual units; and if our intellects had not been organized to thus conceive units, we could talk of an army no way but by repeating the muster-roll; nor would that have sufficed—every soldier, George or Thomas, or whatever may be his name, being himself a unit only intellectually; while physically, he is head, arms, face, eyes, hands, and other multitudinous and almost innumerable sensible items.

§ 2. Arriving thus accidentally and gradually at the knowledge that names, like globe, orange, army, etc., imply a oneness which is only intellectual and *subjective,* while the *objective* things named may be sensibly multiform, I soon found that the analysis would unriddle many questions that have long perplexed metaphysics; for instance, can seeing inform us of distance? When distance is analysed as above, we find a sight distance, a feel distance, and an intellectual conception uniting the two; therefore, whether seeing can inform us of distance, depends wholly upon what we choose to deem the signification of the nominal unit distance. If we limit the signification to the intellectual unit, we may maintain that neither seeing nor feeling can inform us of distance; they only suggest distance to the mind. If, again, we limit the meaning of the nominal unit to the feel distance, we may maintain that feeling can inform us of distance, but seeing cannot. The controversy relates not to unverbal things, but to the definition of the word distance; a question over which we possess an entire control, it being wholly conventional and verbal.

What we have said of the nominal unit distance, we may repeat of the nominal unit figure. Can seeing inform us of roundness? Roundness, as a unit, is a conception of the intellect, while sensibly we find a sight roundness and a feel roundness, as we manifested when speaking of globe. If, however, we choose to limit the meaning of the word to the intellectual unit, we may mystify ourselves and others by affirming that neither seeing nor feeling can reveal to us roundness; or we may limit the signification of the word to the feel roundness, and then astonish ourselves by finding that seeing cannot inform us of roundness.

And what we have thus said of distance and figure, we may repeat of the nominal unit externality. We find a sight external, a feel external, and an intellectual unit, which the intellect forms out of the two sensible manifestations; and to which unit the word external is commonly limited. If, therefore, you limit the word external to the intellectual unit, (excluding the sight and the feel,) you may mystify yourself with the discovery that the earth and nothing therein, possesses an existence external of your intellect; and deem this stupid, worthless, though somewhat famous verbal equivoke, a great psychological mystery. Or should this insidious subtraction of two things from three, and finding only one remain, be too obviously simple to be mystified, you may include the feel in your definition of the nominal unit external, and thereby (still excluding the sight) arrive at the conclusion that seeing cannot inform us of externality; and that without the sense of feeling we should know nothing of the externality of the universe. This latent verbal criticism constitutes, in some of its many phases, what I meant when I said in my first lecture that while philosophers are investigating and determining the meaning of words, they deem themselves engaged in profounder discussions.

§ 3. The nominal unit shadow is an intellectual unit

also, but we never mystify ourselves in relation thereto, for it is as much a unit sensibly as it is nominally and intellectually. The like may be said of echo and of light; but the greater number of nominal units are severally an intellectual aggregation of different and often numerous sensible items; and we may greatly mystify ourselves if we look *sensibly* for their oneness which is intellectual. A city, for instance, composed of a hundred thousand inhabitants, and ten thousand houses, is as much a nominal unit as a shadow; but if we seek the city, deeming it some *sensible* unit that conforms in oneness to the city's oneness which is intellectual, we may deem the ill success of our fallacious sensible search a great mystery. So, if we seek in man for some physical or sensible unit which shall conform in oneness to man's nominal oneness, we are, in like manner, seeking physically for what is not physical but intellectual. Such searches are deemed neither fallacious nor futile, and much has been written to determine in what part of physical man his oneness consists. If you cut off Peter's arms, the remainder of Peter will be a man. Take off his legs, and his remainder is still a man; how much, therefore, say such inquirers, and what must you take away from Peter before the remainder will cease from being a man?—thereby evidently mistaking the nominal oneness, which is only intellectual, for a physical mystery.

The nominal unit matter is mysterious from a like misapprehension of the nature of its oneness. All we know thereof, say philosophers, is the sensible properties of matter; what the unit matter itself is, remains, like man's oneness, among the unsolvable mysteries of life. Why? Because, in neither case can our senses discover any such unit. Of course they cannot, for it is not sensible, but only intellectually conceived. But how do I know the unit matter is merely an intellection? Because, what our senses cannot discover, cannot be sensible, and must of necessity be intellectual, if we know it at all. Well did Bishop Berkely say, in reference to speculations of this kind, whose latent verbal sophistry he saw partially, that men first raise a smoke or dust, and then complain that they cannot see. The delusion by which the intellectually conceived unit matter is thus looked for among the sensible items which compose the physical meaning of the word matter, and the intellectually conceived unit man among the various physical parts which compose the physical meaning of the word man, is analogous to the ancient puzzle, denominated sorites: a heap of wheat is exhibited to a person, and you proceed with him among the individual grains to look for the heap itself. You take up a grain and ask him if that is the heap? You proceed thus with every grain, till the whole will be exhausted, without finding the heap, for the heap alluded to is an intellection.

What is individuality, what is magnetism, what is vitality, what is madness, what is fever, what is gravity, what is electricity, etc.? The questions are asked continually, and they presuppose that each of the nominal units names a physical unit, to whose mysterious subtility (not to the fallaciousness of the search) is attributed the sensible undiscoverability of the unit in each case. Whether medical science suffers or not by deeming fever and each other nominal disease a physical unit, merits the consideration of physicians. Many medical theories seem to owe their origin to this error. But not only fever in general is not a physical unit, the particular fever of Thomas is not a physical unit. It consists physically of many sensible manifestations; and if we would escape delusion, we must deem their nominal oneness the result of only an organic operation of our intellect; an operation which is as useful as it is inevitable; but we need not gratuitously engraft on the utility a mischievous error, by deeming the oneness physical when it is only intellectual.

What we have said of fever, we may repeat of contagion. The oneness which pertains to contagion is only intellectual. The contagiousness of cholera generally, and the contagiousness of any single case of cholera, are severally alike in oneness; but the sensible unverbal manifestations that the intellect thus aggregates in each case into a verbal unit, may be more multiform in one case than in another, and they may differ otherwise. Even the contagiousness of a single case during its whole continuance, is less a unit physically than its contagiousness on any given moment; hence to investigate the contagiousness of cholera, and to proceed by supposing that the contagiousness possesses unverbally the oneness which the word contagiousness purports, is like seeking for magnetism as a physical unit among all unverbal magnetic phenomena. It is seeking *objectively* in unverbal nature for a unit that exists only *subjectively* in the intellect.

The health of a country is as much an intellectual unit as the health of Thomas. Unverbally the oneness of the two cases is incalculably dissimilar. Even Thomas's general health during a year is less an unverbal unit, than his health at the present moment. The saltness of the ocean is an intellectual unit, and the saltness of any given drop of the ocean is another; but the saltness of the ocean is sensibly multiform, while the saltness of the drop is as much a unit sensibly as intellectually. The oneness of an army is intellectually as much a unit as the oneness of Napoleon who commands it; while sensibly their oneness is very dissimilar.

I trust the examples given are sufficient to manifest that the name of every physical thing implies a oneness which is only intellectual; and that when we mistake the nominal oneness for a sensible or physical oneness, we are deluding ourselves with an indiscrimination as bewildering as it is fallacious. These remarks are applicable to all names of physical things, from the universe, which is the most comprehensive of nominal units, to a shadow, that is as much a unit physically as it is intellectually and nominally.

Of Moral Units.

§ 1. But all nominal units are not intellectual aggregations of sensible manifestations. Most, if not all those which we have been considering, are such; and I have, therefore, denominated them physical units. But as the intellect creates such physical units out of certain sensible manifestations, so the intellect creates the nominal unit *love* out of certain unverbal manifestations of our internal feelings; and this unit love, with all other units that relate to our internal feelings, I shall denominate *moral units,* and sometimes emotional units. If we turn from words to unverbal things, we find that a man may be said to love music, his dog, his horse, his wife, his dinner, his child, his business, and innumerable other physical things. He may love reflection, metaphysics, mathematics, and numerous other intellectual things. He may love ease, excitement, pleasure, revenge, and numerous other internal feelings; but if amid the numerous and divers unverbal feelings to which we thus apply the word love, we look for love itself, and suppose it to be some mysterious unverbal unit, we are looking objectively for what is only a subjective creation of the intellect. That every language contains the nominal unit love, is scarcely to be doubted, and the coincidence is conclusive that the intellect conceives the unit by an organic necessity; but if we mistakenly deem this intellectual conception a mysterious emotional unit, or a unit of any kind, except in the conception of the intellect, we are needlessly mystifying our knowledge, and it is sadly thus mystified, unless I greatly misjudge.

§ 2. What we have said of love we may repeat severally of envy, hate, malice, hope, fear, conscience, piety, religion, faith, kindness, passion, rage, charity, and every other nominal unit that refers to internal feelings. Every man's consciousness, embracing his knowledge of his own personality through the course of his past life, is supposed to possess as much unverbal oneness as it possesses nominal oneness; while, like each of the former units, it is the name of an intellectual aggregation of multitudinous units, just as the wealth of a man is the name of his aggregate pecuniary possessions.

But the mystery which proceeds from mistaking the true unverbal character of the implied oneness, is greatly aggravated when we endeavour to find a corresponding unit anywhere except in the organism of our intellect; and especially when, in any case, we imagine that the intellectually conceived unit is physical. Such speculations are, however, no way uncommon. In treatises, for instance, which have been written on our passions, appetites, emotions, etc., the multitudinous internal feelings which give significancy to the word love, are enumerated, not as the meaning of the word love, but as the propensities of a mysterious unit love, who holds his seat in the heart. So in some treatises on our intellectual powers, wisdom, reason, judgment, conscience, and numerous kindred intellectually conceived nominal units, are crowded into the head, where, as on invisible tripods and in specific localities, they sit and hold dominion over the conduct, thoughts, and feelings of the man in whom they are situated.

3. To a person who is destitute of internal feelings, (if

we may for illustration imagine such a person,) the nominal units love, hope, fear, etc., would possess but little unverbal meaning; as also joy, sorrow, anger, jealousy, hunger, thirst, sleepiness, weariness, vigour, lassitude, etc. The words would not, however, be destitute of unverbal meaning to him, because nearly every such nominal unit includes within its signification some sensible external action or appearance, which enables us to determine by looking at a man, that he is sleepy, faint, angry, jealous, envious, hungry, etc. By means of these external exhibitions, a man who should be void of internal feelings, might discourse about love, anger, envy, etc.; as a man void of the sense of taste could talk of the deliciousness of peaches, oranges, grapes, etc., his words referring to the appearance of the fruits; or, as a man void of sight could talk of the delightfulness of sunshine, his words referring to the warmth of the sunbeams.

Of intellectual operations aggregated into nominal units.

§ 1. I could easily give, to any extent, examples of units that, like the foregoing, the intellect forms out of our internal feelings. I have designated them moral units, moral being usually applied to the branch of our organization that is neither physical nor intellectual. But the intellect converts also into units its own operations, and to these I now wish to direct your attention. I hope you understand what has already been said, and you, doubtless, understand numerous operations that you see daily, and numerous things that you feel hourly, and numerous griefs and joys that you are conscious of; but the understanding itself, as a *unit*, is only a nominal creation which the intellect forms in contemplation of the various unverbal acts of understanding to which I have referred. The intellect, likewise, (of which I speak so often as a unit,) is itself only an intellectually conceived aggregation in all that relates to its oneness, as separate and different from the various intellectual operations that we are conscious of experiencing. The like may be said of mind, sagacity, judgment, reflection, reason, wisdom, wit, cunning, and all other nominal units that refer to unverbal intellectual operations, and whose names occupy no small space in our dictionaries.

§ 2. What is truth? said Pilate. His question implies that he deemed truth a unit, and the question is supposed to be as proper and profound now as Pilate deemed it; truth being still deemed a mysterious unit. If, however, we turn from words to unverbal things, we find many and different truths. That a line not longer than an inch, may be divided ad infinitum, is a mathematical truth; that I am speaking, is a physical truth; that honesty is the best policy, is an ethical truth; that you have felt grief, is a moral truth; that an unsupported stone will fall to the earth, is an experimental truth; that heaven and earth shall pass away, is a religious truth; and that the matter of a grain of sand may be logically divided interminably without arriving at a residue which cannot be further divided, is a logical truth. We may enumerate millions of truths;

but if we look among them for truth itself as a unit, we are looking for a figment which the intellect forms organically and of necessity; and which unit is *subjective,* not *objective,* in the organism of the intellect alone, not in objective things.

Nominal units that are partly intellectual and partly moral.

Before I close in relation to nominal units, I must speak of some whose signification is not wholly sensible manifestations, nor wholly emotional manifestations, nor wholly intellectual manifestations; but internal feelings, associated with intellectual conceptions. I allude to Deity, immortality, eternity, heaven, hell, angel, resurrection, soul, and numerous other kindred nominal units. The existence of such nominal units in all languages, and in all periods of time, is proof unequivocal that the intellect is organized to conceive them; and hence that they all possess a *subjective* reality in human nature. Of their conception by the intellect, and their unverbal signification, I shall speak in another place; but at present, I speak of them in relation only to their nominal oneness, in contrast with their unverbal multiplicity.

All the last mentioned nominal units derive their chief cogency from certain internal feelings which may be designated as religious feelings, and which, in some cases, constitute the entire objective signification of the intellectually conceived units. Such feelings are as indissolubly a part of every man's organism as hope, fear, doubt, conviction, confidence, uncertainty, etc. The whole history of man manifests the existence of religious feelings, and every particular man's consciousness demonstrates their existence occasionally. A man may not at all times be under the influence of religious feelings, any more than he is at all times under the influence of hope, fear, love, or aversion; but he is always liable to the excitation of religious feelings, as he is to any of his other feelings.

When we are unacquainted with the above twofold character (intellectual and moral) of the nominal units we are speaking of in the present section, we may be surprised at the levity with which some persons regard them, in contrast, with the awe with which other men regard them. A principle analogous to this we may discover in the different appreciation which different persons evince towards the nominal units spectre, ghost, apparition, spirit, etc. These nominal units are often associated with an internal feeling that renders each of the nominal units a subject of awe or fear; while to other men they are associated with no such feeling, and may be contemned. But even the nominal units ghost, spectre, etc., seem not wholly creations of the intellect, but to be organically associated with the feelings of fear; and whether any effort of any man's intellect can *at all times,* and *in all places,* wholly disconnect the feeling of fear from the intellectual unit ghost, etc., is very questionable. We are apt to attribute the connected fear to tales which are told us in our infancy; but the foundation exists in our intellectual and moral or ganisms, and an uneducated deaf mute, devoid of all language, may experience unverbally both the intellectual impulse or state, from which the nominal unit ghost, etc., proceeds, and, in association therewith, the internal feeling of fear.

Of nominal units, whose components belong to two or more of the senses, or whose components are otherwise generically diverse.

§. 1. I have said all that I deem necessary to manifest the unverbal multiplicity, etc., of nominal units. The distinction is of the utmost practical importance, and the fault is our own if we continue to mystify and perplex ourselves by seeking objectively a oneness that is only subjective; seeking in unverbal things, a oneness that is only verbal; seeking physically, a oneness that is only intellectually conceived. If any person is tired of the subject, he can omit what intervenes, and proceed directly to the next succeeding lecture; but if he can endure a continuance of the subject, I want to add a few remarks on several collateral topics, and especially in relation to nominal units, like globe, orange, external, etc., of which I spoke at the commencement of this lecture, and which intellectually aggregate unverbal things that are revealed to us by more than one of our senses; and whose nominal oneness is consequently peculiarly puzzling when we seek it sensibly. I want to suggest a mode to speculatists, by which the generic diversity in the unverbal components of any such nominal unit may become sensibly apparent. The alphabet is a nominal unit, and possesses as much intellectually conceived oneness as the letter A; but even the letter A possesses less sensible oneness than nominal oneness; for it names four different sounds. Orthoepists designate which of the four sounds the letter A denotes in any given use of it, by plying over the A some character which conventionally reveals the intended sound. Philosophers might adopt a like contrivance when using any nominal unit that aggregates objects generically different. I, might denote intellection; S, sight; F, feel; T, taste; L, smell; D, sound; G, internal feeling. For instance, *thickness* is a nominal unit, but sensibly I can feel thickness and I can see thickness; consequently, the intellectually conceived nominal unit thickness names a sensible duality. We, however, possess an entire control over the definition of the word thickness, and can define it to signify the *feel* thickness, excluding the sight thickness. This definition is as good as any other when we understand the intended limitation; but we may convert such a limitation into a puzzle when the limitation is not avowed. Professor Reid thus puzzled himself, as follows:—He says, "When I look at a book, it seems to possess thickness as well as length and breadth; but we are certain the visible appearance possesses no *thickness,* for it can be represented exactly on a piece of flat canvass." Now, if he had placed the letter F over the word thickness, so as to denote he was limiting the word to the feel thickness, he would have seen the quibble which arises from saying we can represent thickness on a piece of flat canvass. We cannot represent the *feel* thickness on the flat canvass; we can represent the *sight* thickness only, which is just what we see when we look at the canvass.

§ 2. That seeing cannot communicate unverbally to us the feel thickness, may be an interesting item of experimental knowledge, indicatory of the general truth that each of the senses yields us unverbal information that no one or more of the other senses can yield us; but we need not give the tenet an artificial and sophistical piquancy, by limiting the unverbal signification of the word thickness to the feel, and then asserting that thickness is invisible. No trick of legerdemain is superior in deception to such a dodge, if we may thus designate what is performed ignorantly. The feel thickness, the sight, and the intellection which unites the sight and feel, are three different items of our unverbal knowledge, and entitled to equal honour. We may, if we choose, restrict the word thickness to the feel, and assert that the sight is no part of thickness; but unverbal things are no party to our verbal disquisitions. They exhibit themselves just as our senses and our intellect discover, unaffected by our speculations, unchanged by our definitions.

Hume announces a like unconscious quibble, when he says, "The table (S) which we see, seems to diminish (S) as we recede from it, but the real table (F) suffers no diminution." (F) The whole zest of the proposition consists in the sensible duality of each of the nominal units table and diminution. That the sight table exhibits a visible diminution (S), while the feel table suffers no tactile diminution (F), are no contradiction of each other, the oneness of the table being only intellectual and nominal, not sensible; and we may say the like of the diminution. That the *sight* diminution and the *feel* undiminution can exist thus together, is a physical fact of much interest; but we can make a mystery of it only when we play at bo-peep with words, by neglecting to discriminate the intellectually conceived oneness of diminution, and its physical duality.

The sight crooked, and the feel straight, can also exist together, as we may learn experimentally if we will immerse a straight (F) stick in water, leaving a portion of its length unimmersed. The experiment is interesting, but we can make a juggle of it by neglecting to discriminate that stick, which is a nominal unit, is a physical duality; and that crooked and straight are severally but nominal units, while sensibly each is a duality. With a proper discrimination between the nominal oneness and the sensible duality, no contradiction exists when the sight crooked will, under given circumstances, appear in association with the feel straight. If we suppose that the sight crooked must always be accompanied with the feel crooked, and the feel straight with the sight straight, the error is in our inexperience, not in our senses or in unverbal things.

If a piece of gold is held in front of a mirror, the mirror will exhibit the sight gold separated from the feel. If you look at a candle, and press with your finger against the external angle of one of your eyes, you will experience the sight—two candles, unaccompanied by the feel, two. If you look at the sun, and then close your eyes; or, without looking at the sun, if you press for a moment rather painfully against either of your eyes, you will see various colours, unaccompanied by any of the tangible objects with which colours are generally associated. If you whirl your body and produce dizziness, every object on which you look will exhibit the sight rotation, unaccompanied by the feel. If you cross the third and fourth fingers of your right hand, and rest the tips of the crossed fingers on a bullet, you will experience the feel, two bullets, unaccompanied by the sight two. If a wine-glass be half filled with cotton wool, and immersed (in an inverted position) in a bowl of water, the cotton will exhibit the sight wet, as you slowly emerge the wine-glass; while to the feel, the cotton will be dry; and a wheel can whirl so rapidly and evenly, as to present the feel motion, without the sight.

In concluding this topic, I will add only, that the art of painting consists, principally, in exhibiting sights separated from their usually attendant feels; the sight prominence, without the feel prominence; the sight distance, without the feel distance; the sight shape, without the feel shape. The art of manufacturing perfumery consists in separating the smell rose, jessamine, etc., from the sights and feels with which the smells are naturally associated. Ventriloquism and mimickry consist in separating sounds from the sights and feels with which the sounds are naturally associated. Sleight of hand and natural magic are either the apparent or actual separation of sights, feels, etc., which nature generally associates. Usually some sight separated from its associated feel, as when a juggler apparently places (S) a ball under a cup, but places (F) it not under; and finally, novels, and other imaginative verbal compositions, may be characterised as collections of nominal units, separated from all the sensible things with which the nominal units are usually associated.

§ 3. But though the sensible items are separable of each group which the intellect constitutes into a nominal unit, still so reliably uniform are the groups (as to the several items of which each group is composed), that when, for example, we see space, we know immediately that our hand will encounter no resistance in passing through it; and when we look at glass, we know that our hand will encounter resistance; and when I see ice of a given appearance, I know it will sustain my weight, and I venture on it fearlessly; but when I see water, I know it will not sustain me, and I avoid it carefully. Our sensible perceptions constitute thus an unverbal language common to all men, and more important by far than Latin and Greek; and equally with Latin and Greek, an acquired language, though not a conventional language. A noise which to me originally, and which to an infant is still a mere sensation of hearing, will communicate to me what animal or thing causes it, whether the cause is located in the room where I am sitting, or in a room below me, or above—in the clouds or in the street; and whether the noise is associated with danger or mirth. The noise is become, without any conventionality, a natural word, whose meaning I have learnt experimentally, and whose meaning is understood equally by men of all nations. An ignorance of this unverbal language by children produces much of the intellectual difference that exists between them and adults; and which we erroneously attribute to immaturity of intellect, it being a mere deficiency of sensible experience. A child who is just beginning to walk, will step off a table if you place him on one, the appearance of vacancy yielding him no intimation that it cannot sustain him; and when he begins to run in the streets, horses and approaching carriages appear to his sight as they appear to yours, but the sights yield him no intimation that he will be run over unless he change his position. Should he select a peach from a basket, he will not see, as you can, which is ripe and good flavoured, but probably select one which is big, but which you see is decayed or otherwise undesirable. We exclaim against his stupidity, but his defect is organic, and no brilliancy of native powers can spontaneously supply the experimental knowledge of which he is deficient. We may tell him to grasp the moon, and we may smile when he reaches forth his tiny arm to obey our bidding; but seeing can yield a priori no intimation of what the arm can reach, or what it cannot, except in cases which his intellect sees to be analogous to cases which he has experienced.

The sight of red-hot iron, which so palpably admonishes us to beware of a contact with it, might tempt a child to touch it; and he will see nothing in the point of a needle to indicate to him that a pressure against it is more to be avoided than a pressure against a bullet. A blind man, who should be suddenly restored to sight, would, in the same way, see in a stone wall no indication of its impassability to his hand; and see in space, no indication that his hand will encounter from it no resistance. Such a man would continue to grope his way by means of a stick till he had acquired a knowledge of the unverbal language of which I am speaking; so as to know, by the appearance, where he can tread safely, and where he can move unobstructedly. Every feel, taste and smell, is a natural word as much as the sights and sounds of which we have been speaking. To feel the point of a needle and to feel a bullet will originally no more indicate the sights with which the point and bullet are respectively associated, than the sound of a Greek word will indicate to an untaught man the English word which is its synonyme.

§ 4. Men, however, doubtless differ from each other in the facility with which they *acquire* a knowledge of this natural, unverbal, and unconventional language; and on this difference depends much of what we call dullness of apprehension and stupidity. Men differ also from each other in the extent of their *knowledge* of this unverbal language. A physician can ascertain, somewhat, the condition of a patient's lungs and heart by the sound which the lungs create in respiration, and which the heart produces in its palpitations; but should a man who is not a physician hear the sounds, he would derive from them no information. Every mechanic is acquainted with items of the foregoing unverbal language that are unknown to other men. Some men, by looking for the first time at a picture, can tell, almost unmistakably, the master who painted it; some, by the ring of mixed metals, can tell the constituents of the compound; and some, by looking at cloth, can tell its durability.

§ 5. The world, at different periods, has understood this unverbal, unconventional language in varying quantities. Liquids long expanded and contracted in bulk, ere men learnt from the visible contractions and expansions, that heat and cold were indicated thereby; and the pulse knocked at our wrists for ages, with varying rapidity and intensity, ere men discovered the vital messages the knocks were unverbally telling. Galvani was not the first person to whom the quivering limbs of frogs spoke unverbally; he was only the first person who understood their mute revelations; and, doubtless, around us continually are innumerable unverbal utterances that keep repeating important signs that are still unintelligible to us. Geology is among the latest systematic translations that men have made out of Nature's unverbal dictionary; though the sensible signs which compose geology are as old as man himself. Finally, the unverbal language of which I have been speaking has never received the consideration which it merits, and never has been taught in the way which would lead men to further increase their knowledge thereof. Possibly every sensible perception is a word in the above sense, and to investigate its meaning may lead to greater utilities than the interpretation of any Egyptian hieroglyphic. I will dismiss the subject with only one more remark:—When a house is kindling with fire at midnight, the fact can be unverbally disclosed to us by the smell, the sound, and the sight, in advance of the more fatal information by the feel; so the approach towards us of a person concerns frequently our safety, and it can scarcely be effected so stealthily as not to cause some sound, some visual shade, or some aerial trepidation that will admonish us of the approach; now the remark which I wish to make is, that a like multiplicity of signs, variously modified, seem to attend, somewhat peculiarly, physical operations, whose occurrence concerns our personal safety. Whether a like analogy attends poisonous plants and minerals, so that their presence may be discovered by signs numerous in proportion to the malignity of the poison, I know not; though something similar thereto is discoverable in the sounds produced by rattlesnakes.

§ 6. Having thus seen that sensible things are perceived by us in groups of so uniform an association, that when I perceive any one of a group, the perception becomes to me an unverbal sign of the remainder of the group, we may readily understand why many persons when they see an ignus fatuus, or any other unusual sight of fire, unassociated with a feel, are alarmed at the absence of the feel. The alarm is founded on the indiscrimination which prevails generally between the intellectual oneness of fire, and its sensible duality; hence the absence of the feel seems to prove not merely that the phosphorescent fire is *not* the unit fire which possesses both a sight and a feel, but that it *is* fire portentously disembodied of its feel, and become a species of ghost.

The effect of novelty in sensible associations, as above exemplified, is organic, or the effect would not be apparent, as we find it is, in all men and in all periods of the world. Novelty, though thus agitative of our feelings, is not agitative of the intellect, and we are able to discover a happy utility in this organic exemption from agitation of the intellect. By the passiveness of the intellect, we are fitted to derive knowledge from sensible revelations of every description, and by the excitability of the feelings, we are induced to pay special attention to novelties; and to ascertain whether they are apparent only, or real, necessary or contingent, etc. The effect of novelty ceases, also, on our feelings, as soon as it has accomplished its organic duty. When we become familiar with phosphorescent appearances, etc., we contemplate them with feelings entirely tranquil.

§ 7. But the error of imputing to sensible things the oneness that is only intellectual, and which error thus alarms us when we experience in separation a portion of the sensible items that are usually aggregated by the intellect into a unit, is productive of another error that ought to be understood; for instance, should you place in the hands of an inexperienced person a bladder inflated with air, and another bladder filled with sand, he will suppose that the contents of both possess visibility. He will not pretend to decide whether the contents of both are sapid or odorous; but he will be positive of the visibility; for he has always found visibility associated with tangibility, and he, therefore, supposes the two as much a sensible unit as they are an intellectual unit. Under the like indiscrimination we look at the sun, moon, and stars; and seeing in them shape and visibility, deem them also tangible; just as though tangibility, visibility, and shape, were a physical unit, instead of being only an intellectual unit.

I admit that the appearance of these celestial bodies is strongly presumptive of their tangibility, and that our intellect is organically compelled to conceive that they are tangible; but let us not make our knowledge less definite than Providence enables us to make it; especially as Providence, perhaps purposely to give us a clue to the triplicity of our organization, and the consequent conglomerate nature of words, presents us with just about enough anomalous sensible disassociations to enable us to unravel the three-plied cord with which unverbal things are intellectually tied together by language into nominal units.

§ 8. I have now completed all I deem necessary to say in relation to the unverbal duality or multifariousness of nearly every nominal unit; but in dismissing the subject, I will state briefly how we acquire nominal units, and though the information is not necessarily connected with my discussions, the utility of the information may justify the digression. We are prone to suppose that when our eyes are kept open, nothing more is necessary to the perception of all visible things within the range of our vision; but this is a mistake. Were an unprofessional man to attempt the dissection of a human body, he would see in it but the few nominal units, skin, flesh, bones, etc., while a professional surgeon will see all the units, whose names fill a large anatomical dictionary. To have these multifarious units manifested to him unverbally, constitutes much of a surgical student's professional education. Even now, after all the sensible inspection to which the human body has been for ages subjected, we occasionally hear of some newly discovered unit; as, for instance, the sensible discoveries in the structure of the brain by Gaul and Spurzheim. The surface, likewise, of the earth exhibits to common observers but little more sensible diversity than is referred to by the nominal units ground, stones, trees, shrubs and plants; while educated men see in it the multifarious units which constitute the nomenclature of mineralogy and botany. These sciences are new, and like phrenology, which is more recent, were created by the discovery of units which our predecessors never saw, though as palpably before their eyes as before ours.

§ 9. Every man's intellect individuates (conceives units) in a ratio compounded of the familiarity of his senses with the objects inspected, and of the familiarity of his intellect with the process of individuation; hence children individuate less than adults, being in most cases obstructed by both sensible unfamiliarity and intellectual inexperience. When, therefore, we travel with our children, we are continually calling their attention to objects which will otherwise escape their observation. We attribute their heedlessness to immaturity of age, but a vigorous man would individuate as imperfectly as a child were he as little accustomed to the practice, and surrounded by objects as new. We can discover this in a man who suddenly obtains sight after being connaturally blind. In his first views he individuates neither persons, chairs, tables, carpets, walls, etc., but, like an infant, he sees perhaps the whole as a unit. We are often told by persons who never analyse words into unverbal things, and never discriminate the generic differences of unverbal things, that a restored blind man affirmed that everything seemed to *touch* his eyes. He may have so affirmed, but the affirmation meant nothing but an attempt of his intellect to account theoretically for the new perception. Even all of us account for visual perceptions in the same way, our intellect organically insisting that some rays must pass from the visible object and *touch* the retina of the eye; and thus, like the above restored blind man, we assimilate vision to tactile perceptions; no other mode of perception being satisfactory to our prepossessions in favour of tactile operations. Lord Montboddo made the required contact by conceiving that the soul goes forth from the eye and *touches* the object which is seen; for how can any one object operate on another, we say, except by contact.

§ 10. The defectiveness with which we individuate when surrounded by unaccustomed objects, is so well known practically, that when we are walking with a friend around his grounds, he will habitually direct attention to objects that he may deem most worthy of our notice. By the same principle, when we see a large panorama, the first view is confused, and individuations present themselves only gradually. After a man has viewed daily such a picture for months, he will not see all the units which the artist can see who designed and executed the painting. Also on this principle, likenesses are said to grow on us when viewing the portrait of an acquaintance; for after we have once individuated the points of resemblance, we recur to them again readily whenever we look at the portrait. I have found much difficulty in making children see the eyes, nose and mouth, which most persons see in the full moon; but after these units have been once intellectually individuated in severalty, the child sees them again readily whenever the moon presents them. The difficulty lies in only the first individuation, thus evincing that the obstruction is not in the object seen, but in our organization.

§ 11. The unaptness of very young children to individuate is further discoverable in their usual inability to recognize in a portrait the person portrayed. The portrait will be seen by them as a unit in which they will include the back ground and picture frame; but if they should see only the whole face as a unit, they would not be likely to recognize the likeness, which probably is discoverable in only some of the features individually. Nor is this the whole of the difficulty; for when a very young child looks at the person who is portrayed, the child will not necessarily individuate the face as a unit, but he may include some part of the body and dress. That such are the early individuations of children is known by the fact that a change of head-dress, and sometimes of a gown, will prevent an infant from recognizing its nurse or mother. The like difficulty obstructs a child when we endeavour to teach him by sight, the alphabet. The A, which seems so distinct to us, is to him only a part of a unit whose whole may include much of the surrounding concomitants. No contrivance of ours can obviate his difficulty, though we attempt, more empirically, however, than scientifically, to give prominence to the letter that we desire him to learn, placing it on a square of wood, ivory, etc., or by some other contrivance. Men experience a like difficulty when they hear an unaccustomed language. The words seem all the same sound, till we acquire by time an ability to individuate their sonal differences.

The individuations of men, at all periods of maturity, are much influenced by accustomed occupations. A landscape painter will individuate picturesque views where an agriculturist will see nothing but qualities of soil; and a butcher nothing but the marketable condition of the cattle that are grazing in the fields.

§ 12. The progress of individuations, of which a few instances are above referred to, and the unverbal language of sensible perceptions, still more briefly referred to precedingly, were both indicated to me incidentally while investigating, as I have heretofore stated, the powers of our respective senses; and indeed, to those investigations, began in early life and continued to this time, I have derived all the views of language that I possess; and very much other knowledge that I suppose to be useful. I commenced the investigations with no definite intention, except an assumption that as our objective knowledge of the external universe is derived entirely from our senses, an experimental and minute analysis of the operations of the senses must be useful. I state the fact, and present some of the results, from a belief that such sensible investigations are too much neglected, and in the hope that benefits may result from directing the attention thereto of persons possessing leisure; the mode in which our intellect creates nominal units being not properly the concern of our present disquisitions, but only the mode in which we shall interpret them, so as not to deem their oneness unverbal, when it is only verbal, etc.

LECTURE IV.

VERBAL IDENTITY ANALYSED INTO UNVERBAL DIVERSITY.

CONTENTS.

1. Identity is a subjective conception of the intellect, not an objective perception of the senses.
2. Physical things that are nominally identical, are identical in only the conception of our intellect.
3. Intellectual things that are nominally identical, are identical in only the conception of the intellect.
4. Internal feelings which are nominally identical, are identical in only the conception of the intellect.
5. Language is founded on the two intellectual organic processes of creating nominal units and verbal identities.
6. The latent defects which are inherent in logic, by reason of the foregoing properties of words, and Logic's disregard of unverbal heterogeneities.

Verbal identity analysed into unverbal diversity.

§ 1. Having in my last lecture shown that we impute to nominal units a oneness that is intellectual only, I shall now show that we impute to them an identity that is also intellectual only. This truth was suggested to me, like the former, during my investigations of the powers of our senses, to which I referred in my last lecture. In those investigations I assumed that every sight is unknown to me which my seeing has not informed me of; that every feel is unknown to me that my feeling has not informed me of; and I assumed the like of the information of each of my other senses. Still these apparently obvious truths were contradicted the moment I designated the information of my senses by other names than sights, sounds, feels, etc., for I cannot say that the sight of snow is unknown to me, except the snow that I have seen; that the sight of oranges is unknown to me, except the oranges that I have actually seen; that the appearance is unknown to me of lions, except of the few that I have seen, etc. Endeavouring to reconcile this contradiction between positions that seemed equally irrefragible, I found that all lions are identical; hence when I saw one lion, I in effect saw every lion; and when I saw one orange, I in effect saw every orange.

But this explanation was soon refuted by reflection, for the name lion, etc., is applied to countless individuals who differ from each other in size, colour, and innumerable other sensible manifestations; hence my original assumption was still uncontradicted that every sight is unknown to me which my seeing has not informed me of; the appearance of a lion, orange, etc., which I have not seen, being not necessarily known to me by means of the lion, etc., which I have seen. The name man, also, is applied to many hundreds of millions of the earth's inhabitants who differ in complexion through countless gradations, from negro black, to albino white. Nor is the difference of complexion merely white, black, brown and red, as language implies, the word white being applied to snow, silver, water, the moon, the floor, and other countlessly diverse appearances; and the like may be said of black, brown, red, etc.; hence the unverbal differences of man's complexion, are almost as numerous as the persons. Men differ, also, from each other, not merely in complexion, but in features, stature, hair, age, sex, structure, knowledge, etc.; and each of these words is applicable, like the word white, to multitudinous unverbal diversities; to say nothing of countless unverbal differences in men, that have received no nominal designation. In short, no two men are so much alike unverbally as to prevent them from being discriminated from each other by the appearance; no two speak so much alike as to prevent them from being discriminated by the voice; no two sympathise so much alike as not to differ in their sympathies, appetites, and passions; and no two think so much alike as not to differ in their thoughts and other intellectual conceptions. Still they are all nominally men, and thus all *nominally* identical. One may occupy an imperial throne, and possess refinement, elegance, and knowledge; another may wallow in a gutter, intoxicated, ignorant, stupid, and ragged; but in language like that of Burns, a man is a man for all that; and in this judgment, everybody's intellect irresistibly concurs, thereby implying that a mysterious identity exists that is supreme over all physical, moral, and intellectual diversities.

What, then, is the identity between this multitude of nominal units, man, who severally differ thus from each other sensibly, morally, and intellectually? At one time I supposed the identity was only conventional, and that we arbitrarily designate alike all the unverbally diverse individuals referred to. But how came we to apply the same name to beings so diverse? A reason for the designation must have preceded the designation, for it is applied to these unverbally different beings in all languages, and has been so applied in all ages; and, therefore, is too general for any conventional origin; finally, I saw that as men are not identical in unverbal manifestations, the nominal identity must be only an organic conception of the intellect.

When we become satisfied that the nominal identity is an intellection, we can analyse it no further. We are, in respect to it, at the ultimate reach of our unverbal analysis, like a chemist when he has analysed a compound into its ultimate elements. We may, indeed, investigate the extent to which men approximate to the possession in common of the same unverbal physical things; and the extent to which all men agree unverbally in moral and intellectual manifestations; but if we endeavour to discover sensibly, in different men, the identity which is implied between them by the name man, we are seeking *sensibly* for what is only an *intellectual* conception, and our search is organically absurd and fallacious.

What we have thus said of man, we may repeat severally of horse, elephant, eagle, dog, tree, shrub, whale, heat, cold, blood, light, air, water, fire, and every other nominal unit. Each of the names identifies innumerable individuals that differ unverbally from each other, the intellect alone converting them into identities. In the creation of such identities, the intellect obeys an organic necessity which is as active, I have no doubt, in an uneducated deaf mute as in us; though in him the identity possesses not the objective definiteness which it acquires in us from its connection with an oral name. Could we realize how the intellect of a mute conceives unverbally such identities, we should understand more definitely than we now do, the intellectual organism which gives equal significance to any given conception, whether it be expressed in Dutch or English, in manual signs, or possibly in what may sound to us unmeaning gabble in idiots.

§ 2. By means of the organic action of the intellect which thus verbally identifies sensible and other diversities, the inhabitants of different countries who have never seen the same horses, the same trees, birds, houses, etc., are enabled, when conversing together, to understand each other with sufficient accuracy for all ordinary purposes; unverbal things of the same name conforming to each other with a degree of unverbal similitude, that approximates somewhat to the verbal identity. I lately in France saw a vegetable differing in appearance from any I had ever seen. I accordingly asked the usual question, What is it? and was told it was a melon. The answer gave me much information by reason of my knowledge of American melons, and the further knowledge (or perhaps intuition) that the verbal identity would be accompanied with unverbal similarities.

We see in this intuitive principle of interpretation a reason for the anxiety usually manifested by sick persons and their friends, to know the name of the patient's disease—a desire most urgent, probably, among persons who mistake verbal identities for unverbal identities. Modern physicians, on whom experience forces a knowledge of the sensible diversity that exists among diseases that are nominally identical, are often unwilling to announce to a patient the name of his disease,—diseases nominally identical being accompanied in different patients with fewer unverbal similarities than perhaps any other nominal identities; and even the same person will be affected differently at different times by re-attacks of the same nominal disease. Still some unverbal similarities must exist among diseases verbally identical, or physicians could derive no knowledge from experience. The unverbal similarities of the same nominal disease in different patients is, however, in some few diseases, nearly as complete as the nominal identity of the disease; and in such diseases, experience yields its usual benefits, and medical science exhibits its most reliable ministrations.

Different verbal identities exhibit different degrees of unverbal similitudes.

§ 1. What we have said of the unverbal diversity that exists in diseases of the same name, is measurably applicable to every drug of the same name,—no two masses of calomel, rhubarb, etc., possessing as much sensible similarity as they possess nominal identity. The sensible similarities approximate usefully to the nominal identity, but sufficient diversities exist to embarrass medical practice. Physicians are embarrassed in their speculations, as well as in their medical practice, by the unverbal diversities of verbal identities. The contagiousness of cholera, in different cases, possesses only a nominal identity, while unverbally the contagiousness may possess endless diversities. Even the contagiousness of Peter's cholera to-day, may differ unverbally from the contagiousness of his cholera to-morrow; nothing being necessary to warrant the application of the word contagiousness to any disease at any time, but that the intellect of the observer shall observe in the disease something analogous to what it has observed in some other case that is deemed contagious. We can learn from the controversies of physicians nothing so positive, as that the sensible manifestations denominated contagiousness, are so diverse in diseases of different names, and in diseases of any one name at different times of its occurrence, that to verbally allege contagiousness of any given nominal disease, will communicate to the hearer but little definite unverbal information.

Leaving medicine and its concomitants, we shall find that no unverbal things which are verbally identical, possess as much unverbal similarity as verbal identity; but though the diversity is thus general, it varies in degree in different cases. The sensible similarity in two drops of water is infinitely greater than the sensible similarity of two men, of whom one shall be an uneducated negro, and the other an educated European. But the sensible similarity of the two men is much greater than the sensible similarity of two fish, of which one shall be a shark, and the other an anchovy, while the sensible similitude of the two fish is greater than the sensible similitude of matter in the form of a rock, and matter in the form of a sunbeam.

§ 3. Natural History is irremediably defective to the extent that the nominal identity of animals of any given name conflicts with their sensible diversities. We can construct no natural history, except by speaking of lions as identities, horses as identities, whales as identities, etc.; but we shall gain in unverbal accuracy by understanding that the unverbal objects thus grouped into nominal identities, are identical in only the conception of the intellect; and this remark applies not merely to classifications like the above which the intellect makes spontaneously, but to classifications which are made by naturalists artificially, on any basis whatever.

Books of travels are subject to a like irremediable defect. A traveller describing verbally what he saw in strange countries, can make himself intelligible unverbally to his readers only by means of the intellectual identities to which the traveller's verbal trees will refer; and his verbal rocks, men, and animals, etc.; but the sensible diversities which exist among things nominally identical, make all descriptive verbal narratives very fallacious. When this inherent defect is attempted to be remedied by pictorial representations in books of travels, the defect is less effectually remedied than persons usually suppose. A picture can communicate to a spectator no sight which the spectator has never seen, except the picture itself may be such a sight; but in every sensible particular in which the portrayed view or object differs unverbally from the picture, the portrayed object cannot be revealed by the picture. The difficulty is organic, and cannot be surmounted.

§ 4. The grouping of unverbal things by the intellect into nominal identities, enables us with a few names to discourse intelligibly of innumerable unverbal individualities; the word man, for instance, names, as we have already said, many hundred millions of diverse individuals; and the words dog, tree, fever, grass, meat, drink, etc., name severally numerous and at least equally diverse individuals. If the diverse unverbal individuals referred to by each name, man, dog, etc., could not have been thus grouped into identities by the intellect, and we could speak of them by only giving a different name to each individual, language would have been either impossible, or limited to the designation of a few individuals known in common to the interlocutors; as now when we speak to each other of particular individuals, we can speak of only such as we can bring to each other's knowledge, as Mr. A., and Mrs. B., etc.; hence we discover the very interesting and important fact, that language is constructed on two intellectual processes—the creation of verbal units, (as we manifested in the last lecture,) and the creation of verbal identities, asmanifested in the present lecture. By the creation of nominal units, the illimitable multitudes of unverbal things are grouped into a manageable number of nominal units; and by the creation of verbal identities, the illimitable unverbal diversities of the nominal units, (no two spears of grass being unverbally alike,) are abridged into some few thousand verbal identities; the total number of words, for all purposes, that compose the English language, being only about sixty thousand, though it is, perhaps, the most copious of existing languages.

And we may note as also deserving our recognition, that the above two processes (the creation of nominal units and the creation of verbal identities) are no contrivances of man, no mere conventionality of language, but proceed from an organic impulse of the intellect. The organic proneness of the intellect to note similarities as identities, rather than to note diversities, is readily seen in children. After learning the word cow and the animal so named, they will apply the word to horses as well as cows; and the child's familiarity with animals must be long established before he will discriminate between cows, oxen, and bulls. Nor must we deem such indiscrimination peculiar to children. When a man who is unaccustomed to rural objects, sees a flock of sheep, they will look identically alike, though the shepherd who attends the flock, will know them individually, as accurately as he can discriminate individual men among his human acquaintances. We may note the same organic proneness to identify rather than discriminate, when we look at clouds, and grotesquely form thereout mountains, camels, lions, whales, etc., no man ever thinking what the clouds are not like, but only what they are like. So the first impression of every man when he looks at a portrait, is not whom it is not like, but whom it is like; and, indeed, we may say of pictures as we have said of words, that if the organic tendency of our intellect had been to discover diversities rather than similitudes, we, probably, should have possessed no art of portraiture.

The discrimination of diversities is further unlike the perception of similitudes by requiring usually an effort of the will; hence dull, sleepy, and stupid people, discriminate differences less than persons who are deemed brilliant. The perception of discriminations may be improved by keeping the intellect attentive thereto, and the power is well worth our cultivation. I know a man of ordinary discernment who sat for many years by a wood fire, which was supported on a pair of brass andirons, and he had never seen that the andirons were not matched, till a casual acquaintance directed his attention to a prominent visible diversity in them.

Unverbal diversity of intellectual units that are verbally identical.

§ 1. I have probably said enough to evince the unverbal

diversity that exists in sensible units that are verbally identical. I desire to show a like unverbal diversity among intellectual units that are verbally identical. Every man possesses some wisdom, but if we seek in the several wisdoms of all men for an unverbal identity, except subjectively in the conception of the intellect from which alone the verbal identity proceeds, we are puzzling ourselves by mistaking the nature of the identity. Without this organic intellectual identification of unverbal similarities or analogies, we could possess no such general word as wisdom; let us, therefore, accept the benefit thankfully without making the verbal identification of unverbal diversities a speculative delusion, through ignorance of a distinction which our intellect enables us to understand. And not only is the wisdom of different men not identical, except verbally, but the wisdom of Thomas to-day, and his wisdom yesterday, are only verbally identical, and may be unverbally very diverse. And what we have said of wisdom we may repeat of wit, judgment, sagacity, cunning, discrimination, reflection, anticipation, ratiocination, reason, to the end of the vocabulary of intellectual personages and processes. Each word names countless unverbal diversities, which the intellect alone identifies. The diversities, however, which each word identifies, never perplex us practically; the intellect of any man knowing what unverbal thing to name wit, judgment, cunning, etc., as readily as it knows what unverbal things are fish, insect, or vegetable, etc.

Diversity of internal feelings that are verbally identical.

§ 1. I have shown sufficiently, I suppose, that all intellectual things which are verbally identical, are generally diverse from each other. I will, therefore, proceed to show the like of our internal feelings, and that the anger of Thomas, and the anger of James, which are verbally identical, are identical in only the conception of the intellect. Even the anger of Thomas to-day, and his anger yesterday, are only verbally identical, while unverbally they may differ much from each other. The love, also, which I feel for my dog, my children, property, country, etc., are verbal identities. They possess a sufficient analogy to each other to induce the intellect to deem them identities, under the common name love; just as the intellect sees in a shark, an anchovy, and an eel, a sufficient analogy to deem them identities, under the common name fish; but we shall be deluded in either case, if we deem the verbal identity anything more than a conception of the intellect.

We may apply the foregoing remarks severally, to all other verbal identities formed of our internal feelings, as pride, pity, vanity, glory, shame, generosity, patriotism, goodness, etc. If we contemplate our emotional manifestations ever so superficially, we must see the great diversity that exists unverbally in the goodness of a good ship, a good horse, a good road, a good man, and so of every other verbally identical goodness; to say nothing of the diversity which exists unverbally among a thousand horses that are severally good, a thousand ships, etc. Such identities produce no practical, and but little speculative difficulty, their unverbal diversity being obvious; unless a man more curious than ordinary, begins to speculatively inquire in what the identity exists of these several goods; and fails to discover that it exists in merely an analogy which the intellect discovers between them; and which it discovers so organically, that we know as instantaneously what to designate good, as we know instantly, without any previous acquaintance, what to designate as a metal or a tree.

§ 2. I will only remark further, on the present topic, that the difficulty which men experience in disclosing to each other the precise unverbal feeling that they are experiencing on any occasion, compels us to give the same name to very diverse feelings; while the facility with which we can exhibit to each other sensible objects, enables us to give the same name to only very close resemblances; compare, for instance, the slight sensible difference between any two scarlets, with the great emotional difference that exists between the pity you feel for your sick child, and the pity you feel for a wounded fly. Verbally the two pities are as identical as the two scarlets.

Verbal identities among things other than units or individualities.

§ 1. Most of the unverbal identities to which I have as yet alluded, are what grammarians term nouns, and what I in a former lecture called nominal units or individualities. But the intellect converts into verbal identities, not nouns only, but qualities, actions, and relations of various kinds, etc. Sugar is sweet, honey, fruit of many kinds, etc., are all sweet; but if we look for the identity of the several sweets, except in the organic perception of the intellect to which alone the verbal identity owes its origin, we shall not understand language correctly. So fire is hot, sunshine is hot, our hands are sometimes hot, the atmosphere may be hot, etc.; but if we look for the identity of these several hots, except in the intellect, in whose conception alone the identity exists, we shall not find it.

In the creation of such verbal identities, the intellect obeys an organic impulse which is irresistible; and the intellect seems equally compelled to subsequently aggregate such identities into nominal units; as, for instance, to aggregate the several hots into the nominal unit caloric, and the several sweets into the nominal unit sweetness, and certain particular sweets into a unit under the name of saccharine; but when we fail to understand that such verbal identities and nominal units are intellectual, not physical, we needlessly neglect a discrimination which also the intellect is organized to make. The conception of the identity and the unit are both useful, but a correct understanding of the identities and units is equally useful, our organization evolving utilities in all its capabilities.

§ 2. But not only the sweets of sugar, honey, fruit, etc., are only verbally identical, but some unverbal diversity may exist in the sweet of different sugars, as it certainly exists in the sweet of different oranges, different apples, etc. The like may be said of the identity of every nominal quality. Snow, salt, silver, glass, water, the moon, my hand, and this paper, are all verbally white, for the intellect sees an analogy in their appearance; and to that intellectual conception the word white refers; but if you seek among the numerous whites for a sensible identity that shall conform to the verbal identity, your search is fallacious. Even the white of different waters, different glasses, or different snows, is not usually in any one class of the articles as complete unverbally as verbally.

Perhaps every man will occasionally think of his personal identity and sameness. He is conscious that he is the same being, now, perhaps, decrepit and old, that was once an infant, once a youth, once a vigorous man. He is the same man, who is kind and amiable to his wife and children, and perhaps harsh and hateful to other persons. He is the same man, who was once innocent and happy; now perhaps guilty and unhappy. He exhibits his portrait, and beholders smile when he assures them it was once a correct delineation. He looks in a mirror and is himself shocked at the change which time has produced in him; he reflects on his feelings and is surprised how calmly he contemplates events that once overwhelmed him with grief; and how indifferent he feels towards death and other future contingencies that once agitated him with apprehensions. He is changed in his physical aggregate, and in every physical particular—he is changed morally in the intensity of every feeling, and intellectually in almost every opinion; still he can no more doubt his sameness and identity amidst these changes, than he can doubt his present existence. His sameness is an undiscoverable and perplexing mystery while he attempts to discover it physically; but it ceases from being mysterious when he knows that it is only a conception of his intellect, and hence that it no way conflicts with the countless sensible diversities he has suffered. Indeed, the only proper mystery to every man is his own organization, for all other mysteries are solvable thereby as in the foregoing example. His own organization is somewhat like the ocean. He can account for rivers, creeks, and springs, by the descent of rain from the clouds, and he can account for the rain in the clouds by evaporations from the ocean; but the ocean yields no explanation of its own exhaustless fullness, rolling and heaving incessantly, and leaving nothing for us but to note and wonder.

§ 3. The verbal identity which exists thus between qualities, etc., that are very diverse unverbally, we often employ to add a piquancy to our intellectual speculations. Stone, we say, is material, air is material, light, water, earth, and iron, are severally material. We are then taught to wonder and admire that sunbeams thus identical with iron and stone, can fall with a velocity unparalleled, and from a height of millions of miles, and not merely leave our houses unbattered, but leave us unconscious of the blows which are inflicted on even our eyes. Now I would ask why, in such recitals, are we fond of directing our attention to the velocity of light and the height from which it falls. Our motive clearly is to thereby manifest that our eyes ought to be hurt. But why ought they to be hurt?—simply because we identify light with stone. With the intellectual identification of the two, I wage no controversy; but I would fain dispel the error which proceeds from not discriminating unverbal differences in things verbally identical. The verbal equivoke is pleasing to the feeling of wonder in I suppose every man; but as we no longer tolerate necromancy, except when it is avowed to be sleight of hand, I think we ought no longer to tolerate intellectual identities to be presented to us as physical identities. Let us enjoy all the benefits that proceed from the organism by which our intellect identifies verbally, diversities that are unverbal; but let us not vitiate the benefits by unnecessarily disregarding generic and other unverbal diversities in things verbally identical.

I lately saw a book intended for the instruction of youth, in which the reader's curiosity is sought to be excited by the information that he and iron possess many qualities in common, as colour, form, substance, mobility, etc. So far as the qualities are verbally identical, the child knows the identity; but so far as you want him to deem the identity physical, instead of an intellectual conception, you are deluding him with an equivoke. Youth are taught that plants are male and female. The verbal identity thus established between plants and animals, is a conception of the intellect, founded on certain analogies which the intellect organically sees between plants and animals, and I admit they are many, and highly deserving of observation; but when we desire a youth to confound the intellectually conceived verbal identity with a physical identity, we are creating an interest for botany at the expense of his and our own understanding. The difference is just what it is between intellectually conceived vegetable sexuality and animal sexuality. By commenting on the verbal identity of the two sexualities, I desire not to commit the error that I am seeking to dispel; that is, I desire not that their difference shall be estimated by my words, or by any words, but simply by the unverbal differences that are discoverable between them; and especially by not confounding the information we receive from our intellect and the information we receive from our senses; the two informations being generically different.

§ 4. Leaving as sufficiently explained, the verbal identity of qualities of the same name, I will examine the verbal identity of certain relations which grammarians call prepositions. Colour is *on* (Sight) grass; a carpet is *on* (Feel) the floor; a fragrance is *on* (Smell) a leaf; a word is *on* (Intellection) my tongue; an eclipse is *on* (Sight) the moon; a burden is *on* (G) my conscience. That the inteltellect insists on thus identifying these sensible diversities, arises from the beneficial organic necessity of which we have already spoken as one of the essential bases of language. Still we need not vitiate this benefit by deeming the verbal identity antagonistic to the unverbal diversity of the several cases: puzzling ourselves to discover *physically* how colour can be *on* grass as a carpet is *on* a floor. Professor Stewart, labouring under this puzzle, says, "The bias of every person is certainly to deem that the green colour of grass is spread on grass as a carpet is spread on a floor." The bias is, I admit, general, and as inevitable as general, and as unsophistical as inevitable, for it is intellectual; and signifies merely that in the conception of our intellect the colour of grass bears the same relation to the grass as a carpet bears to a floor on which it is spread; but the conception involves no negation of the physical differences that can be discovered in the two cases; as, for instance, that the carpet can be felt as something apart from the floor, while the colour cannot be felt apart from the grass. Unverbal sensible diversities result necessarily from the diversity of our senses; and when we subsequently arraign the sensible diversities at the bar of our intellect, and confront them with their verbal identity, as conceived by our intellect, we are trying the sensible diversities by standards that pertain to the intellect, and to which the sensible diversities owe no fealty.

I at one time thought that language is chargeable with originating misconceptions like the foregoing, and that we ought to have designated by different names the sight *on*, and the feel *on*, etc.; but the difficulty underlies language, or all languages would not make identities of such sensible differences. A deaf mute who knows no language, will intellectually deem the colour of grass to bear the same relation to the grass, as a carpet bears to the floor over which it is spread; and he may not understand that the identity of the relation in the two cases, is only a conception of the intellect; hence when he reflects that the carpet can be felt apart from the floor, while the colour cannot be felt apart from the grass, his intellect may not discern that the physical diversity of the two cases is no antagonist of the intellectual identity.

What I have thus said of the numerous unverbal diversities that the intellect verbally identifies by means of the word *on,* I might repeat of the numerous other unverbal diversities that the intellect verbally identifies by means of the words here, there, out, in, etc. My hand is *in* a glove, a haze is *in* the atmosphere, heat is *in* fire, an odour is *in* roses, hardness is *in* iron, sweetness is *in* sugar, a thought is *in* my mind, etc., etc.; but I will refrain from the repetition, nor will I show that every verb and parti ciple identifies verbally unverbal things that are diverse, precisely as the above prepositions on and in, identify verbally what unverbally are diverse; for if what I have already said is not sufficient, I cannot make plainer that the unverbal diversities which exist in things verbally identical are not contradicted by their verbal identity; the verbal identity being subjective and relating to the intellect, while the unverbal diversities are objective, and relate to unverbal things. Such of my readers as comprehend this puzzling distinction, may omit what intervenes, and proceed to the next succeeding lecture; though the intervening remarks, especially those on the inherent defects of logic, will well repay the labour of a perusal, unless I misjudge the amount of knowledge which exists on the nature of language;—I much solicit a perusal of the whole.

§ 5. I will, therefore, close the present lecture by exhibiting a few miscellaneous verbal identities, whose unverbal meanings are not merely *diverse,* but *heterogeneous.* Lecture II. treated of things that are verbally homogeneous, but unverbally heterogeneous; and I shall now reproduce some of the examples which I therein adduced, though I shall now produce them to exhibit their verbal identity in contrast with their generic diversity. The *passage,* for instance, of light from the sun to the earth is an intellectual conception, not a sensible perception, like the *passage* of a steamboat from Albany to New York. Our senses perceive that light ensues on the earth when the sun rises above the horizon; but we see only the sensible sequence of the sun and light, not any *passage* separately of the light, as we see the *passage* separately of a steamboat through the water. No man can, however, prevent his intellect from identifying the two passages; but when we permit the verbal identity to mystify and delude us by our deeming the identity objective instead of subjective, we become astonished, and may even thereby well suspect that we have wandered from the sober realities of the senses, into the fairy land of the intellect. But as we compare together the physical passage of a steamboat, etc., and the intellectually conceived passage of light, for the purpose of astonishing ourselves by the contrast, why should we not relieve the astonishment, by showing that the two passages are only verbally identical, though unverbally diverse; one being sensible, and the other intellectual. Just as well may we mystify ourselves by asking, how the soul is *united* to the body? how heat and light are *united* in flame? how coldness and hardness are *united* in ice? how the movements of a man's limbs are *united* to his volition? how effects are *united* to causes? how sweetness is *united* to sugar, and an echo *united* to a sound? Well, all these questions have been asked from the earliest periods of speculative inquiry, and they are still asked. The difficulty is just like the foregoing. Two links of an iron chain are united by a sensible union, but the union of the soul to the body, etc., is an intellectual conception. If, however, we suppose that the intellectual identification of the two unions authorizes us to seek in the soul and body, etc., for a physical union, like what our senses perceive in two links of a chain; or to make a mystery of our inability to discover sensibly such a union; we are utterly misunderstanding, not language only, but our perceptive organization.

The error assumes a thousand different phases, and I am striving only to manifest it, not to chronicle the errors in detail. We teach a child that certain stars are suns. We court his belief that the identity is not intellectual merely, but as unverbal as verbal, despite the sensible diversity, which only gives a zest to the sophistical identity. Our inability to account for the luminousness of certain stars, except by assimilating them with the sun, induces the intellect to make the assimilation; and we possess other inducements; but the assimilation, however induced, is intellectual, and will excite no feeling of surprise in any person when thus understood. Beyond all natural visibility and all telescopic, other suns we say exist, orb above orb without end; still wishing the child to continue the erroneous indiscrimination between the verbal identity which is intellectual, and the unverbal diversity that is physical. With the logic that produces such intellections I have no controversy; though I ought to say here as a complement of former incidental remarks on the same subject, that the defect of logic consists in its taking no cognizance of the heterogeneity which exists in the unverbal meaning of words. This defect renders the conclusions of logic wholly unreliable in all speculative disquisitions not purely intellectual; and of this I will subjoin an example in the succeeding paragraph, which quotes Zeno's celebrated paradox in relation to motion. Nothing can be more practically important than for us to understand the foregoing inherent defect of logic; and I believe it has heretofore escaped detection. Till a man understands it, he is in constant danger of becoming the victim of some speculative delusion. Creation needs no logical equivokes for its exaltation, nor the perversion of reason for its glory. We tell a youth that the earth travels with various velocities, and gyrates in different circles; but the youth is deceived by the verbal identity, when he believes that the intellectually conceived gyrations and velocities are unverbally identical with physical gyrations and velocities; and that he is physically whirled through space momentarily, some thousand miles in one direction, and some seventeen miles in another.

Zeno's celebrated paradox respecting motion, to which I alluded above, is as good an example as I can adduce, of the wonders we may logically produce by not discriminating unverbal diversities among things verbally identical; for instance, admit that a tortoise is a mile before Achilles, and that Achilles runs a hundred times faster than the tortoise, yet Achilles will never overtake the tortoise, though he continue the chase forever; "because," says Zeno, "when Achilles has run the mile, the tortoise will have moved forward the hundredth part of a mile; and while Achilles runs the hundredth part of a mile, the tortoise has moved forward the ten-thousandth part of a mile; so that it is not yet overtaken. In the same manner whilst Achilles passes over the ten-thousandth part of a mile, the tortoise moves on the millionth part of a mile, and is not yet overtaken; and so on ad infinitum." The millionth part of a mile leaves them asunder say about the fifteenth part of an inch, which is a physical distance; hence the tortoise is, as stated, not yet physically overtaken. But the next nominal progression will create a necromantic quibble, unless we see that the words no longer retain a physical meaning, but are speaking of intellectual conceptions; for instance, Achilles is distant from the tortoise the fifteenth part of an inch, and the tortoise is not yet overtaken; but while Achilles pursues the tortoise along this fifteenth part of an inch, the tortoise will move forward the fifteen-hundredth part of an inch; and is, therefore, by the terms of the proposition, not yet overtaken. But the fifteen-hundredth part of an inch, or some more comminuted progression, will possess only an intellectual signification; and if we deem it a physical separation between Achilles and the tortoise, we are deluded by the verbal identity that exists among things unverbally and generically diverse.

In the same intellectual way, no limit exists to the divisibility of matter; for every nominal whole possesses intellectually two nominal halves, and each nominal half becomes immediately, when separately considered, an intellectual whole, endued with nominal halves; and so ad infinitum. The logic is incontestible, and the conclusion is true intellectually, and true, physically also, while the words possess any sensible signification; but after a certain number of sensible divisions of any sensible thing, the word half will refer to neither a sight nor a feel, and will become as physically insignificant, and as purely an intellectual conception only, as the insensible distance which separates Achilles from the tortoise; hence the defect is alike in the logic of both propositions. So little understood, however, is the defect, that the infinite divisibility of matter is treasured as a physical truth; while Zeno's kindred problem, (from interfering more grossly with our physical experience,) is called a quibble.

The intellect may imagine a circle that shall be verbally larger than the orbit described by the earth in its annual revolutions, still no part of the imagined verbal circumference can be verbally a straight line; for no proposition in mathematics is more logically satisfactory, than that a nominal straight line cannot constitute a nominal circle; hence we arrive logically at the intellectual conclusion, that a curve may expand ad infinitum without becoming straight; though at every verbal expansion of the curve, it approximates intellectually towards verbal straightness. In view of this logical process Hume says, "the demonstration seems as unexceptionable as that which proves the three angles of a triangle to be equal to two right angles; though the latter opinion is natural and easy, and the former big with contradiction and absurdity. Reason here seems thrown into a kind of amazement, which, without the suggestion of any sceptic, gives her a diffidence of herself, and of the ground on which she treads. She sees a full light, but it borders upon the most profound darkness. Between them she is so dazzled and confounded, that she can scarcely pronounce with certainty concerning any object."

But the difficulty vanishes if we discriminate the unverbal diversity that exists among verbal identities, and which diversity logic disregards. Mathematicians are correct physically, so long as the words which they employ refer to sensible existences; but when they speak of a curve which can neither be seen nor felt, it is a verbal curve minus a physical curve; and the proposition is like the problem of Zeno—that is, the names curve, circle, etc., refer to only intellections. If we deem them unverbally identical with the physical things of the same name, we are confounding things that are unverbally diverse. When we see a juggler cut a hole out of our handkerchief, and subsequently restore to us the handkerchief uncut, we know he has deluded us, though we may be unable to discover how; so when we see the logical processes to which Hume refers, we ought to know that some delusion exists, though we should be unable to explain what the delusion is. The subject merits any amount of further illustration, but I am attempting the manifestation of only principles.

PART II.

OF THE UNFALLACIOUS INTERPRETATION OF LANGUAGE.

LECTURE V.

OF THE UNVERBAL SIGNIFICATION OF WORDS.

CONTENTS.

1. The nominal identity of any two or more unverbal things must be interpreted by their unverbal diversity.
2. The verbal homogeneity of any two or more unverbal things must be interpreted by their unverbal heterogeneity.
3. The nominal oneness of any verbal thing must be interpreted by its unverbal multiplicity.

Of the unverbal signification of verbal identities.

§ 1. I have completed all I contemplate saying on the structure of language, and I am to speak now of the interpretation of words into unverbal things; remembering always, that I have nothing to say about language, except in its relation to unverbal things. The word man is applied to many hundred millions of individuals who severally differ from each other. Their verbal identity proceeds from an organic contrivance of the intellect, and the contrivance is one of the essential foundations of language; but we must necessarily reverse this intellectual contrivance when we want to know what the word man means unverbally in any particular application; that is, the man himself, unverbally, is the only proper exponent of the verbal manhood which our intellect gives him in common with hundreds of millions of other individuals. Courts and juries are often engaged in deciding whether a person is sane or insane. If the intellect of the triers sees an identity between the person's conduct, etc., and other conduct which they deem insane, he will be adjudged insane; but after this decision, we must interpret his adjudged verbal insanity by his unverbal conduct, etc., if we would know what the verbal insanity signifies unverbally in the given case. Ten thousand men may severally be insane at the same time and place, but the identity of their insanity is only an intellectual conception; while, unverbally, their insanity may differ in every individual. Every man is verbally a sinner, but this general admission refers to only an intellectual identification; if you would know what sin is unverbally in any given instance, the instance alone with its unverbal utterance can yield the only proper answer.

Water is fluid, air is fluid, quicksilver, light, blood, electricity, lightning, ether, magnetism, fused iron, are all fluid. The word fluid is correctly applied, for the intellect discovers among the unverbal things thus referred to, a similarity which justifies the application to them of the word fluid; and we may apply the word whenever our intellect discovers that the name is appropriate; but we must not afterwards interpret the unverbal fluidity by the name which we thus attach to it; but the name must, in every case, be interpreted by the unverbal fluidity to which it is attached. Like remarks are applicable to every word.

Again, when we employ the word water to designate the colour of a diamond, the word means the unverbal colour to which the word refers; and the unverbal colour is the only proper exponent of the meaning of the word. When a physician says your blood is watery, the word means the unverbal things to which he refers; and till you are made acquainted with them, you will not understand the physician's unverbal meaning, though you may know the unverbal meaning of watery in every other use of it. Why the colour of a diamond should be designated by the word water, my intellect readily understands, for it sees an analogy between the colour of a diamond and water; and no doubt the intellect of a physician, who applies the term watery to the blood, sees some analogy between the properties of water and the unverbal thing to which he refers when he says a patient's blood is watery.

One of the most beneficial powers of the intellect is the countless multitude of unverbal things that it organically assimilates, thus enabling us to designate all of them by a single word. The more a man's intellect possesses this analogizing power, the more acute we deem his power of generalization; and perhaps man's capacity in this particular, is one of the chief particulars in which he is intellectually superior to other beings. The organic defect of idiots may consist in the deficiency in some idiots, and in the absence in some others, of the powers to conceive identities among unverbal things, and to aggregate unverbal things into units; these two powers of the intellect being the main foundations of language, and the absence or defectiveness thereof would account for the inability among idiots to acquire, employ, and understand language. My opportunities have never placed me in a position to note idiots; but if the above suggestions shall prove to be accurate, they may be useful in the attempt to instruct idiots; the organic powers alluded to being improveable by effort where the powers are not wholly absent.

We discover by the foregoing remarks, that the diversity which exists in the unverbal meaning of even the most simple word, is as great as the diversity of unverbal things among which the intellect can discover a given analogy; hence we can see the necessity of seeking the unverbal meaning of every word in the unverbal thing to which it is applied in every given application. Every word is somewhat like a mirror. The mirror reflects the image of every object that is placed before it, and every word reflects the unverbal things to which the word refers. My hand is red, blood is red, hair is often red, the moon is sometimes red, fire is red, and Indians are red. The intellect sees in these several unverbal sights, an identity or congruity that makes the word red appropriate to all of them; but if you would know unsophistically the unverbal meaning of the word red, in its application to my hand, to an Indian, to the moon, etc., you must, in each application, seek the meaning in the unverbal things referred to. If you look in a dictionary for the meaning of red, the dictionary can give you only the verbal meaning of the word.

Still, after my intellect shall decide that a given colour is red, your intellect may decide it is crimson, for every intellect conceives its own identities or similitudes; but whatever propriety or impropriety may exist in the name with which I designate the colour, the unverbal colour is the only proper exponent of the unverbal meaning of the word; and with this understanding, the unverbal meaning is the same, though fifty different persons call it severally by fifty different names. If, therefore, the persons altercate in reference to the name, they should understand, that so long as they refer to the same sight, their altercation relates to language, not to unverbal things. Whether a given colour shall be called red or crimson, depends on usage, and I shall be verbally wrong if I designate as red what good usage designates as crimson; but people generally discriminate so little between words and unverbal things, that disputants rarely understand definitely whether they are differing verbally or unverbally. I have heard of men who cannot tell "one colour from another," but I have never been able to understand whether the alleged defect is an inability to discriminate differences unverbally, or only an inability to discriminate verbally as other men discriminate, who are skilled in the proper use of words; though the two defects are essentially different, one relating to words, and the other to unverbal things.

§ 2. To remedy as far as practicable the foregoing vagueness in the unverbal meaning of verbal identities, men conventionally define what unverbal things shall constitute the meaning of the words insanity, sin, fever, contagion, knowledge, matter, truth, etc.; but though such definitions are useful, they are all obstructed by the illimitable diversity of unverbal things; and if we would know accurately the unverbal meaning in any given case, of even the word murder, we must interpret the word by the unverbal actions to which the word refers in the given case. If this be true of the word murder, on whose definiteness the life of prisoners is daily either saved or lost, how much greater must be the necessity of thus interpreting the unverbal meaning of ordinary verbal identities, on whose definiteness of unverbal meaning no important consequences are dependent.

Men have, however, succeeded usefully in the substitution of artificial identifications of given animals, vegetables, minerals, etc., in place of the assimilations thereof which the intellect makes spontaneously; and to which ordinary language refers, by the words fish, birds, beasts, trees, shrubs, grass, etc. Still to these scientific identifications, we must apply what we have said above of other definitions; that unverbal things are no party to our nominal classifications, divisions, and subdivisions. Over our language we possess unlimited control: we may designate a whale to be a fish, or not a fish, as we shall think best; but unverbal things remain uncommitted thereby, and precisely as our senses reveal them, as unverbally diverse individually, as they are individually numerous.

§ 3. Having thus shown that verbal identities must be interpreted by their unverbal diversities, I will further illustrate the principle by showing that we often erroneously estimate unverbal diversities by their verbal identity; not seeing that the identity is subjective, not objective, in our intellect, not in the things contemplated by the intellect. The matter, for instance, of which air is composed, is so expansible, that a closed bladder, flaccid and apparently empty, will expand by heat so as to become full and hard. The matter of gold is also very expansible, and a very small piece can be beaten so as to equal in surface a rood or more of land. But these are nothing in comparison with matter in the form of musk, which is so expansible by exposure as to fill with its particles many rooms, while the musk will exhibit no sensible diminution. Light, however, exhibits the expansiveness of matter to a still greater advantage. Its particles are so attenuated that they fall millions of miles, and with a velocity so wonderful as to accomplish the descent in an instant; still they hurt not the eye, though they alight immediately on that susceptible organ. They seem absolutely imponderable, for philosophers have in vain endeavoured with the nicest balances to discover in them any sensible weight, even when the number of particles thrown into the scale have been multiplied by the most powerful lenses.

The above experiments are all interesting unverbally, but what astonishes us in them is a verbal fallacy. If a particle of gold should fall millions of miles in an instant of time and strike our eye, the hurt would be fatal not to the eye only, but to the whole body; still a particle of light will not be even felt by the eye; and we are taught to believe it is not merely verbally identical with the particle of gold, but identical unverbally, except in its greater physical attenuation.

But let us review for a moment the insidiousness with which the artificers of these verbal mysteries aid the delusion by the manner of announcing them. When we are to be astonished by the diffusiveness of odour, it must be announced as an example of the expansiveness of matter. To exhibit it as an example of the diffusiveness of odour, would be only the exhibition of a commonplace fact, no more curious, and no less than any other common occurrence; but the assimilation of the diffusion to the expansion of gold, stone, or other tangible body, is the marvel and the fallacy. The intellect sees the identity of the two, and easily falls into the delusion that is spread for it, of not discriminating between the verbal identity, (which is only an intellectual conception,) and a physical identity; and thus prepared, receives with a gusto the crowning wonder, that the musk remains undiminished in size, notwithstanding the number of rooms it has filled to overflowing. The verbal identification of the diffusiveness of the odour and the expansiveness of gold, produces thus a seeming miracle in comparison with which the physical increase of the Galilean loaves and fishes is as nothing; for no number of baskets can contain the increase of even a single grain of musk.

So again with light. We require some preliminary preparation before the feeling of astonishment can be elicited in us, in relation to what is almost momentarily familiar to our perceptions. We are usually prepared for the forthcoming fallacy by being told that light is composed of material particles, which *materiality* we deem as unverbally identical in light and stone, as it is verbally identical. We are then in a condition to feel astonished that particles of light should not hurt the eye whose peculiar delicacy is usually artfully adverted to; together with the distance which the particles fall, and the velocity of their descent; and then comes the crowning wonder in relation to the expansiveness of matter, that the nicest balances can discover no weight in sunbeams, though concentrated on the balances by the most powerful lenses. The unverbal facts, though abundantly interesting, are accounted as nothing, (that light is innoxious to the eye, and that sunbeams will produce no trepidation in the nicest scales,) but the interest in the narrative is the fallacy, that the *materiality* of light and stones is as identical unverbally, as it is verbally.

We astonish ourselves in the same fallacious way when we talk of communications by an electric telegraph. The electric fluid will travel, we say, from Buffalo to New York with about the celerity of thought. The language is understood with entire accuracy in ordinary intercommunications between man and man, for both speaker and hearer interpret it by the unverbal manifestations to which the language refers; but wholly different is the result when we turn upon language and speculatively interpret the unverbal manifestations of the electric travel by their verbal identity with the travel of a stage-coach or the flow of water. We overlook the fact that the identity of the two travels is *subjective,* not *objective,* in our intellect, and not in sensible realities.

We cast into a tub of water a small piece of indigo, and the water becomes tinged with blue; we cast into another tub of water a lump of sugar, and the water becomes sweet; we open our shutters, and light becomes perceptible throughout our room; we ignite a few sticks of wood, and the mercury will rise in a distant thermometer;—these results possess a certain congruity to our intellect; hence in reference thereto, we say, the indigo and sugar are *diffused* through the water; the light and heat are *diffused* through the room. If, however, we wish to discover the objective unverbal meaning of the word diffused, in these several uses, we must resort to our senses, not to our dictionaries, which can give us only the relation which a given word bears to other words. The unverbal objective meaning is so diverse in the above different applications of the word diffused, that a blind man will possess no knowledge of the diffusion that refers to the light and indigo; while a man who never possessed tasting, will possess no knowledge of the diffusion which refers to the sugar.

§ 4. Verbal identities I shall now dismiss with one important inferential remark, that as the correct unverbal signification of a word is the unverbal thing to which the word refers, every man can interpret words, unverbally, by only the unverbal things that are known to *him;* consequently, my unverbal meaning of a word is unknown to a man who has never witnessed the unverbal thing to which I refer. The analogy which the intellect organically sees between unverbal things of the same name, remedies this latent defect to a good practical degree; but the endless disagreements and controversies which arise among men, in even ordinary conversation, evince that the irremediable difficulty in the unverbal meaning of words is still embarrassing to no small extent.

Nor is the above the only difficulty. The most simple word that can be used, say white, names, even when restricted to sights, innumerable diverse unverbal sights, from the white of snow to the white of an egg, the white of a floor, or the white of a man's hand. The identity between them is only intellectual and verbal; hence when you designate something to me as white, the chances are innumerably great against my receiving from your communication the objective sensible information to which you refer. These defects of language are all inevitable, but to know them is providentially within our power. The defects are, as we shall see below, attended with compensatory benefits, as are, probably, all organic defects; but the evils that proceed from our needless ignorance, are, in this case, as in most others, unmitigated by any advantage.

Of the unverbal interpretation of verbal homogeneities.

§ 1. We are informed in Holy Writ, that after the Creation, God brought all things to Adam, that Adam might name them. To enable Adam to accomplish this task, his intellect had been so organized, that comparatively few things had to be brought to him—his intellect deeming identical innumerable things, notwithstanding their sensible diversities; hence, many things unverbally diverse, became identical in name. Of these verbal identities I have just spoken, and shown the speculative errors into which they betray us in relation to unverbal things. We cannot, however, admire too much the exceeding simplicity and efficiency of the organic intellectual contrivance, by which the innumerable host of unverbal things were thus comprehensible by a number of words not too large for our memory; and men were enabled to talk understandingly to their fellow men, though the interlocutors may never have seen the same horses, the same lions, the same trees, etc. We honour men too much when we deem language a human contrivance, which it is no more than walking, dancing, hopping and jumping, laughing and crying.

But man was designed to commune with himself, and with his fellow men, about not merely such unverbal things as are sensibly perceptible, but about such also as his intellect can conceive; and which latter could, of course, not be brought to Adam that Adam might name them; as, for instance, conceptions about his personal origin, the origin of all other perceivable things, their prospective duration and final catastrophe, their insensible uses in the universe, modes of operation, connections, dependencies, relations, etc. His intellect was accordingly organized to meet this difficulty also, and by a contrivance as simple as the former; that is, the intellect was organized to conceive its notions in words that possess a sensible signification, and to recognize in the conceived words the intellectual notion to which the words refer. Intellectual conceptions acquired thus a *verbal* homogeneity with sensible perceptions, notwithstanding their *unverbal* heterogeneity. This twofold meaning, sensible and intellectual, which the same word may express, is well exemplified in our ideographic numerical figures—the digit 2 expressing a French word to Frenchmen, a German word to Germans, and an English word to Englishmen; or, perhaps, the twofold meaning of the same word may be still better exemplified by Chinese printed words, which we are told are ideographic, and alike intelligible to several nations whose vocal languages are entirely dissimilar.

The verbal homogeneity of intellectual conceptions and sensible perceptions produces no embarrassment in our social intercourse, for when A tells B that cause and effect are *linked* together, B's intellect organically recognizes the intellectual conception to which the word link refers, and is entirely satisfied. But far different is the result when we turn upon language speculatively and insist that causes and effects are not linked together, for our senses can see no link. We forget that the verbal homogeneity between intellectual conceptions and sensible perceptions is merely an organic contrivance, by which alone we can communicate to each other our intellectual notions, and that, consequently, when we would know, *objectively,* what a word means, and whether it means an intellectual conception, or a sensible perception, we must interpret the word by the unverbal thing to which it refers. This, then, is the tenet which I desire to establish in view of the homogeneity of unverbal things. As verbal identities, heretofore alluded to, must be interpreted by their unverbal diversities, and as nominal units must be interpreted by their unverbal duality or multifariousness, so must the verbal homogeneity of unverbal things be interpreted by their unverbal heterogeneity. Language is compelled to deem unverbal things homogeneous, as it is compelled to deem certain unverbal things identical, and certain unverbal things units; but when we would know what the verbal homogeneity means unverbally, in any given case, the unverbal thing alluded to is the only interpreter of its own unverbal generic character.

Such being the general principles which must govern us in disintegrating the verbal homogeneity of things generically heterogeneous, I will illustrate the principle by some few additional examples, though probably further illustration is superfluous. Light and colours pass *through* solid crystal, sound passes *through* a solid block of stone, electricity passes *through* a bar of iron, a thought passes *through* the mind, a pain passes through our head. These several "passages through," differ from the passage of a thread through the eye of a needle, the latter being a sensible perception, while all the former are intellectual conceptions; but if we fail to understand this generic difference, and deem all the passages as homogeneous unverbally, as they are verbally, we may become as needlessly surprised that light can pass through solid crystal, and sound through solid stone etc., as a man would be if he were assured that a linen thread can pass through solid stone, or, as he may be, that he cannot see the link which unites cause and effect. To avoid, therefore, all such delusions we must interpret the *verbal* homogeneity of all "passages through," by their several *unverbal* manifestations and generic differences; but we seem fond of deeming the fallacious homogeneity a mystery of nature, and rather willingly, I suspect, refuse to recognise the generic difference between what is *intellectually* conceived, and what is *sensibly* perceived. Professor Brown says, "That light, itself a body, should pass through *solid* crystal is regarded by us as a physical wonder." Now, if Professor Brown had not been pleased with the verbal equivoke, he would not have increased its pungency by adding the word *solid* to the crystal; the added solidity only leading us to infer, that light, "*itself a body*," ought to be unable to pass through the crystal—the *solid* crystal. Like the foregoing are the expressions, an odour strikes my olfactory nerves, light strikes my retina, a sound strikes my tympanum, a hat strikes my fancy, a project strikes my mind. In ordinary conversation, the intellect of the hearer recognises the intellectual conceptions to which the several strikes refer, and language fulfils therein its proper intention; but when we speculatively interpret the expressions by deeming them *generically* like the expressions, a stone strikes my hand, the wind strikes my face, etc., we surprise ourselves by the fallacious verbal homogeneity that is imputed to the different strikes;—and especially that light can *strike* our retina blow upon blow, and we not feel it.

"Some of the ablest philosophers in Europe are now satisfied," says Professor Stewart, "not only that no evidence exists of motion's being produced by the contact of two bodies, but that proof may be given of the impossibility of such a process." In relation to this discovery, I want to make a few remarks:—When I see a billiard ball move forward on being struck by another billiard ball, I see nothing but a sensible sequence of two sensible events, the stroke and the motion; or, say the contact and the resulting motion. In addition, however, to the sensible contact, and the resulting sensible motion of the struck ball, my intellect conceives a power or causal efficiency in the stroke or contact, to account for the motion that ensues. But, says Professor Stewart, the ablest philosophers of Europe are now satisfied that contact is not the cause which moves the struck ball. Before we can understand, correctly, this remark of Professor Stewart, we must ascertain whether it refers to the efficiency of the stroke, which causes the motion of the struck ball. I suppose such to be his meaning, and that the philosophers mean only that the efficiency referred to, exists not in the sensible contact or stroke. I will, any way, assume such to be the meaning, as the assumption will enable me to say what I desire to communicate in relation thereto. The philosophers are, therefore, I say, only labouring under the common delusion of not knowing that the efficiency which they are alluding to, is merely a conception of the intellect, and, of course, the intellectually conceived efficiency exists not in the contact of one ball with the other, nor in the stroke of one ball against the other. When philosophers are unacquainted with the above simple truth, they are constantly prone to interpose some imaginary causal efficient between the contact and the resulting motion; and we will assume that they shall interpose in the above case, as Professor Stewart alleges, a "power of repulsion," as something which surrounds every particle of matter. All that is gained thereby, is a name for the intellectually conceived causal efficiency; and if they suppose that the "power of repulsion" is a physical existence, we may say of it, as we say of the contact and stroke, that when a billiard ball moves forward on the approach towards it of a certain "power of repulsion," we see nothing but a sequence of two sensible events,—we see the "power of repulsion," and the resulting motion of the billiard ball, but we see not the causal efficiency which is attributed to "the power of repulsion," and which compels the motion that sensibly ensues.

From not knowing, however, that all causal efficiency is only a conception of the intellect, subjective, and not objective, philosophers are constantly striving, as in the above case, to materialize the efficiency of causation, without ever being able to arrive at an end of the process,—every imagined physical efficient, call it a power of repulsion or what else you will, becoming immediately, as we have shown above, only a new sensible antecedent in some sequence; and we can immediately say of every such new antecedent, as we say of the first, that we see only a sequence of sensible events, not the causal efficiency which makes one produce the other. For instance, Locke, in speaking of ice, says that a man would discover a great, but hitherto unknown secret, who should find the cement that holds together, so firmly, the water of which ice is composed. But, adds Locke, this discovery would aid but little, unless he could discover also, the cement which holds together the particles of the cement. To this, I add, that the last-named discovery would still leave undiscovered the cement that holds together the particles of the latter cement, and so on ad infinitum;—every new cement requiring a cement as much as the first, so long as we fail to see that we are vainly endeavouring to materialize a causal cement that is not material, but only a conception of the intellect.

This error is, I think, the source of nearly all our theoretical causal imaginings. We mistake an intellectually conceived causal efficiency for something that is physical, and vainly endeavour to imagine some physical agency that will supply the exigency of our error. The causal efficiency is subjective, and we seek it objectively;—it is in the organism of our intellect, and we seek it in what is sensibly perceptible, or in some imaginary thing analogous thereto; and hence we can keep predicating causes ad infinitum, and are no better satisfied than when we began.

§ 2. The true interpretation of the words of all languages is the unverbal things to which the words refer. That mode of interpretation gives to the intellect what is intellectual, and to the senses what is sensible; while our present indiscrimination of generic differences leads us to conclusions so necromantic, that without any other proof, we ought to know that we are in error. The motion of the earth, for instance, around its own centre at a speed of a thousand miles an hour, and around the sun at a speed of about a thousand miles a minute, are all intellectual conceptions against which I have nothing to say; but when we deem the revolutions and speed, etc., *physical,* we are deluded by the homogeneity which exists verbally between things that unverbally are generically different.

That men exist on the earth whose feet are diametrically opposite to ours and whom we term antipodes, I have no wish to deny as a general proposition; but certainly a generic difference exists between the sensible appearance of men in the imagined position, should two men stand thus before us, and the intellectual conception of the local relation which men bear to each other when they stand on opposite sides of the earth. My intellect will insist on identifying the two cases, the said sensible and the said intellectual; but my intellect enables me to conceive also, a difference between the sensibly perceived antipodal position and the intellectually conceived antipodal relation. Now, all I demand in the premises is, that the two cases shall not be interpreted by their verbal identity, but, on the contrary, the verbal identity shall be interpreted by the unverbal diversity, be it more or less. I think this is not our usual mode of interpretation in the above cases, and that the intellectually conceived local relation which men bear to each other when they stand on opposite sides of the earth, is esteemed in proportion as it is interpreted to be unverbally identical with a picture representing two men in an antipodal position. I comment more particularly on the verbal identity of the above two cases, because a learned friend, to whom I stated the position, saw nothing in it but hypercriticism.

People speak also of seeing distant objects by means of pictures painted on their retina, and seem to be unconscious that they are talking of only an intellectual conception. This, too, my learned friend, above alluded to, deemed hypercritical. I avail myself of his objection, that I may make my meaning more intelligible. I desire not to controvert, as he supposes I do, any sensible perception which is referred to by the alleged picture on the retina; but when a man curiously puzzles himself by supposing that a sensibly perceived landscape is sensibly identical in some way with a miniature picture which his intellect conceives to exist on his retina, his puzzle consists in deeming the identity sensible when unverbally it is only an intellectually conceived identity. If you ask me to say further what the difference is, I say that the equivoke possesses an unverbal piquancy which manifests the difference better than it can be manifested by words.

In relation, however, to the picture itself, I by no means admit that its intellectually conceived existence on the retina of a living man is identical unverbally with its sensibly perceived existence in a dissected eye. The intellect conceives the existence of the picture on the eye of a living man, and the reasons for the conception I cannot question as to their intellectual cogency; but still the intellect can recognise also a demarcation between its conceptions and sensible perceptions; and to understand the unverbal demarcation will certainly not vitiate our knowledge. So far, also, as the intellectually conceived picture is part of a modus operandi by which external objects are conceived to be seen sensibly, I intend not to comment thereon; but if we deem the modus operandi more than an intellectual conception, especially if we fail to discriminate it from sensibly perceived operations, we are confounding things generically different, though they may be verbally homogeneous. All, however, that I demand in the premises, is that the interpretation of the words alluded to shall be governed by what is unverbal in relation thereto; and especially that we shall not interpret what is unverbal by the words that we employ thereon.

Some years ago an ingenious account was published in our country of discoveries made in the moon by an enlarged and improved new telescope. The narrative verified sensibly all that the intellect conceives of the moon in subjective explanation of the moon's sensible appearances. The mountains, chasms, and human inhabitants of the moon were no longer merely intellectual conceptions, for the telescope revealed them sensibly with numerous collateral sensible appendages. Most persons thought that such a sensible realization of existing intellectual conceptions, made the narrative probable; but the accordance in a case like this, and of a kind like this, satisfied me that the narrative was as intellectual merely as the theory which was thus sought to be materialized. My skepticism shocked many persons who never discriminate generic differences in verbal homogeneities, but time soon manifested that the narrative was a hoax. But I have been asked why I spontaneously disbelieved the narrative, since I admit that it only realized sensibly what is universally conceived intellectually. The answer is simply, that an intellectual anticipation of a sensible discovery is reliable as to its sensible realization, just in proportion as the anticipated sensible discovery is analogous to some known sensible occurrence. If I see a bird sitting in a nest, the intellectual conjecture that eggs are beneath the bird is so reliable that a disappointment in the verification of the anticipation would surprise me. Should I, however, see a quadruped lie in his lair, and see an egg under him, my intellect might conceive that he produced eggs, but a sensible realization of such a conception I should deem much less likely than its disappointment; and I estimated our conceptions in relation to the mountains, volcanoes, chasms, etc., of the moon just as little likely of a sensible realization as the conceived production of eggs by a quadruped. The only incredulity which I feel in relation to the recent pendulous experiments at Paris, proceeds, as in the above moon hoax, from their accordance too physically with the intellectually conceived diurnal revolution of the earth; though the experiment, if verified in full, will only add an additional sensible fact to those which are already comprehended under the subjective theory of a diurnal revolution of the earth.

§ 3. In concluding what I have to say of our interpretation of words that relate to things generically different, I want to adduce a few examples from philosophical experiments, wherein we are continually playing, by means of words, a game of bo-peep with unverbal things: at one moment our words referring to *sensible* perceptions, and at another moment to *intellectual* conceptions, etc. When, for instance, you exhibit a prism, you may assert that the light which enters on one side of the prism is composed of the gorgeous colours that are emitted on the other side. The language refers to a theory by which the intellect accounts for the prismatic spectrum; but we desire the spectator, and ourselves included, to interpret the language by deeming the light sensibly alike on both sides of the prism, despite our eyes which affirm the contrary. The only physical interpretation which is not sophistical of such an experiment, is the precise unverbal perceptions of the senses. When, however, we desire a theoretical interpretation, we must accept it in such words as the intellect will suggest; for the intellect organically theorises in words, and the existing theory in relation to the spectrum may be the best that can be conceived. The unverbal meaning of theories and other verbal conceptions of the intellect I shall discuss in another lecture. That such conceptions possess a meaning that is unverbal, we may know from the fact that deaf mutes when uneducated and void of all language, still evince all kinds of intellectual conceptions. The intellect of such a mute may conceive, as well as ours, that ordinary solar white light bears the same relation to the prismatic coloured rays, as a monochromatic cord bears to the variously coloured strands of which the cord may be fabricated. He may also be as much deluded speculatively as we, by not understanding that such a conceived relation between the cord and the light differs *generically* from a sensibly perceived identity.

But after the foregoing prismatic experiment, the experimenter may tell you, that as you have seen a ray of light untwisted by the prism, and split into its constituent threads, he will collect the filaments and retwist them into their original form. With this preface which is true intellectually, but fallacious when interpreted sensibly, he will cause the coloured rays to pass through a lens which will converge them to a foçus of light in its usual colour. The experiment is interesting, but what the observer sees constitutes all the unverbal sensible signification that the experimenter's language possesses.

The intellect seems organically compelled to conceive some theoretical rationale to account for all that our senses perceive; but we need not confound such intellectual conceptions with physical things, nor should we confound them, except for a bias which also seems organic in us towards the excitation of the feeling of wonder in ourselves and others. This bias crowds with spectators all exhibitions of sleight of hand, and probably we should look with but little interest on a prismatic spectrum were we not stimulated by the verbal and hence delusive homogeneity of the intellectual twisting and untwisting of light, with the physical twisting and untwisting of the strands of a rope; and hence imagining that light is somehow sensibly coloured while it looks white, and somehow sensibly white while it looks coloured.

When a chemist ignites a stream of hydrogen gas and oxygen, and permits the flame to pass through a glass tube, the inside of the tube becomes suffused with water. The chemist will accordingly say, that water is *nothing* but a union of the two gases; and intellectually the chemist is right. He is right physically also, to the extent that his language is to be interpreted by what is sensibly perceptible in the experiment; but without being captious, I believe that such an interpretation of the language employed is not intended by any body. I feel an irresistible repugnance myself to such a limitation of the meaning. I want to deem the water gases, and the gases water, in a sense different from the experiment. I want somehow to dispel the sensible diversity of the water and gases, and to substitute therefor as sensible, the identity between them that the intellect conceives. To interpret what is sensible in the experiment by simply its sensible manifestations, takes from the experiment all its piquancy and necromancy.

Chemistry also analyses bodies, and out of glass produces sand, alkali, etc. "Now," says Mr. Brown, (Philosophy of the Mind, Lecture IX.,) "these processes of chemistry enable us only to discover what are always before our eyes; but our sight is not keen enough to see them." That the sand is present in glass, and would be visible were our eyes sufficiently acute, means not the same as when I say this table is present. The word present, as used by Mr. Brown, refers to the intellect which theoretically accounts for the analytical production of the sand by conceiving that the sand is present in the glass. If we see not the generic unverbal difference between a *sensible* presence, and an *intellectually conceived* presence, the equivoke will necessarily surprise us.

"When a spark," says the same philosopher, "falls on gunpowder, and kindles it into explosion, every person ascribes to the spark the power of kindling the inflammable mass. But," continues he, "let any person ask himself what he means by the *power* which he imputes to the spark? and without contenting himself with a few phrases which signify nothing, let him." What? shall he content himself with no phrase, but deem the word power significant of precisely the unverbal things to which the word power is applied? No; he must content himself with some phrases which Mr. Brown prescribes. Such has always been the advice of philosophers, and such will be their advice till they know that the unverbal signification of every word is neither more nor less than the unverbal things (sensible or intellectual as the case may be) to which the word refers. Every philosopher gives us a new phrase, and like a quack with a new nostrum, desires us to be content with no other.

In the present case, Mr. Brown advises the person to answer, that by the power imputed to the spark, he means only, "that in all similar circumstances, an explosion of gunpowder will be the immediate and uniform consequence of the application of a spark." You may suppose that the occurrence is vastly simplified by the new phraseology, but the supposition is founded on the error of employing the phrase to interpret an unverbal occurrence, instead of employing the unverbal occurrence to interpret the phrase. So long as the two phrases refer to the same unverbal occurrence, their unverbal meaning must be the same; but if an explanatory phrase refers to some unverbal thing that is different from the unverbal occurrence referred to by the phrase which is sought to be explained, the parties are controverting without understanding that they are probably referring to unverbal things that are generically different—one of the parties referring to an intellectual conception, and the other to a sensible perception. Most of the controversies of philosophers are founded on such a misunderstanding of the unverbal import of their words.

§ 4. We talk of mountains in the moon, of the tidal influence of the moon, the size and distance of the moon, etc., with no apparent consciousness that we are talking of only *intellectual* conceptions, not of *sensible* things; and that the physical meaning of each expression is limited to only what our senses can perceive, and that the remainder of the meaning is intellectual. But I have said enough of the unverbal interpretation of such verbal homogeneities, and I will proceed to explain the proper unverbal interpretation of some verbal homogeneities whose unverbal heterogeneity consists of internal feelings and intellectual conceptions, instead of consisting, like the foregoing, of sensible perceptions and intellectual conceptions. A man, for instance, may disbelieve in ghosts, and yet be unable to pass alone at night across a burial-ground without fear of ghosts. Can he thus both believe and not believe at the same time? Experience evinces that unverbally he can, and the contradiction is only verbal. One belief may unverbally be intellectual, and the other unverbally an internal feeling. Nothing is more common than the co-existence of such generically diverse beliefs. A man's *intellect* may, like Pyrrho's, believe confidently in the logical non-existence of an external sensible universe, and still on the approach towards him of a coach and horses, he may be compelled by his *feelings* to seek safety in a change of position. Many men disbelieve intellectually all the tenets of Christianity, and still tremble like Felix, while hearing of "righteousness, temperance, and judgment." Such, no doubt, was the position of many Greeks and Romans in relation to the theology of their era; though by interpreting the word belief as something wholly intellectual, we often say that men like Cicero could not possibly believe in the heathen mythology.

§ 5. If we possessed no unverbal belief but what is intellectual, our condition would be wholly unreliable, for the intellect must assent to its own logical deductions; and nothing is so absurd, when interpreted physically, as some of the intellect's conclusions. Even while I am penning this lecture, one of the judges of our Supreme Court publishes gratuitously and ostentatiously, his belief in table-turnings by spiritual agency, and in table-rappings as personal communications by the dead of past ages. He says he believes the above because his intellect can discover no other solution of what his senses have witnessed. Now this judge, though still exercising well his judicial functions on life, liberty, and property, is accounted insane by most men; but in what consists his insanity? In being governed by his intellectual belief, and not by the feeling of unbelief which, in such matters, would govern him, as is supposed, were he in a condition of sanity.

Some time ago, a sect called Millerites in our country, began to preach that the millenium predicted in the Bible, was at hand; and as a precursor thereof, that the earth was soon to be burned up, and "the heavens were to melt with fervent heat." The texts of Scripture on which the predictions were founded, Christians had always assented to; but the moment this sect began to make their intellectual belief therein so effective over their conduct as to abandon their ordinary occupations in preparations for the millenium, they were deemed insane for not being governed by the feeling of unbelief which all sane men are deemed to experience in reference to the immediate advent of the millenium; how much soever the intellect may be able, as in the case of the Millerites, to logically demonstrate that the advent is to be immediate. Our unverbal belief seems to have been given us as a providential corrective of our indiscrimination of the heterogeneity which exists unverbally between intellectual conceptions and sensible perceptions. The intellect may be deceived by verbal homogeneities, as in the above examples, but our internal feelings will not yield to the delusion, and will control our conduct despite of our intellect. The moment, however, we understand the unverbal difference between things verbally homogeneous, we are no longer dependent for our protection on the insubordination of our feelings, for we know that what the intellect conceives is not physical, and that the intellect can reveal to us, in cases like the foregoing, nothing but its own subjective notions.

Having thus endeavoured to show, but perhaps too briefly, that all verbal homogeneities must be interpreted by their unverbal heterogeneities, I will dismiss verbal homogeneities, and proceed to discuss even still more briefly, the last topic of the present lecture.

Of the unverbal interpretation of nominal units.

The nominal oneness of a man is only a conception of the intellect; the nominal oneness of a ship, an army, the universe, magnetism, attraction, matter, life, insanity, fever, gravity, body, etc., are severally only a conception of the intellect. If an army could not be spoken of as a unit, and we could speak of it only by repeating its muster-roll; and if no soldier on the muster-roll could be spoken of as a unit, and we could speak of him only by repeating the skin, flesh, bones, etc., of which he is composed; language would be impossible, or almost useless if possible. But the necessity for aggregating sensible multiplicity into nominal units for the purposes of language, forces us to segregate into its sensible components any given nominal unit, when we would interpret unsophistically what the nominal unit means unverbally. If, on the contrary, you seek sensibly in any such nominal unit for an unverbal oneness that differs from the unverbal multiplicity that you may sensibly perceive therein, you may gain the pleasure of much mystery, but you will lose the benefit of understanding aright the nature of language, and your unverbal knowledge; the oneness which you are seeking sensibly, being only a conception of the intellect.

What we have thus said of the unverbal interpretation of physical units, we may repeat of the unverbal interpretation of intellectual units, as wisdom, wit, imagination, judgment, intellect, truth, knowledge, mind, etc., to the end of the vocabulary of intellectual units. The oneness of each is only intellectually conceived and verbal, while unverbally each unit is as multifarious as its unverbal manifestations; consequently we must segregate the unverbal components of each verbal unit when we would know what its verbal oneness means unverbally. We must practise the like mode of interpretation with every emotional unit, as anger, revenge, jealousy, love, suspicion, vanity, envy, malice, pride, etc., the nominal oneness of each being only a conception of the intellect, while unverbally it is multifarious. Finally, I doubt much if every speculative mystery may not be solved by the foregoing lecture. Ourselves and everything within our consciousness is, in one sense, mysterious; but the peculiar mysteries which perplex our speculations, arise from our misinterpreting nominal *units,* nominal *identities,* and verbal *homogeneities.* Such speculative mysteries all vanish when we interpret verbal homogeneities by their generic unverbal elements, sensible, intellectual, and emotional; and when we interpret verbal identities by their unverbal diversities, and nominal units by their unverbal multiplicity. But I fear, notwithstanding I tautologize these eminent truths in various ways, I shall fail to make them intelligible.

LECTURE VI.

OF THE UNFALLACIOUS INTERPRETATION OF AFFIRMATIVE GENERAL PROPOSITIONS.

CONTENTS.

1. The generality of a proposition is subjective and refers to the intellect; but the objective signification of a proposition is governed by the objects to which it refers.
2. Every general proposition possesses as many different objective significations as it refers to different objects.

§ 1. The propositions of which only I wish to speak either affirm something or deny something; and I shall speak first of affirmative propositions. Twice two are four. Four what? Four anythings to which your intellect may see the proposition is applicable. Every proposition possesses thus two heterogeneous meanings, one general and looking to the intellect, like "twice two are four;" the other particular and looking to the object to which the proposition refers, like twice two apples are four apples. The generality of a proposition is subjective, not objective; hence, general propositions are intellectually what ready-made coats are physically that we find in slop shops. Owing to the physical similarity of men, a coat which fits one man will fit multitudes of men; and owing to the similarity which the intellect sees among objective events and things, the proposition which is intellectually applicable to any objective event or thing, like the foregoing twice two are four, will apply to numerous objective events and things. When, therefore, Pythagoras affirmed that the earth revolves around the sun, we are not compelled to believe that he knew, objectively, what Copernicus subsequently taught thereof, or what the proposition signifies objectively now by means of the developments of Newton. Pythagoras may have meant something intellectually analogous thereto, but which is no part of the existing Newtonian system of the universe. All Pythagoras discovered was the general proposition, "that the earth revolves around the sun." His proposition is an intellectual surtout, which is found to fit many objective bodies that were probably wholly unknown to Pythagoras.

By means, however, of the above objective indefiniteness of subjective general propositions, no modern discovery is announced but some person will show it was known to the ancients; for he will adduce some ancient general proposition that will intellectually fit the modern discovery. Should my Lectures ever gain public attention, many persons will recollect some general proposition of Plato, Socrates, or somebody else, that will intellectually include all that I shall manifest; and in this subjective way alone is the adage true that "nothing is new under the sun." Steam is powerful, dangerous, and useful. This proposition may have been asserted of steam centuries ago, and the proposition would have referred to objective facts then known, that would have made the proposition objectively significant; but we should mistake were we to suppose that the author of the proposition necessarily knew the modern appliances of steam: he may have known none of them. When Lord Bacon recommended physical investigations, we may see from his Novum Organum, that the recommendation was a subjective intellectual garment whose objective occupants were almost worthless; but we speak of Bacon as though his recommendations possessed the same objective signification to him as they possess to us.

Since the time of Newton, his general proposition of universal gravitation includes many objective facts that were unknown to him. So the late experiments with a pendulum, in the Pantheon at Paris, may give additional objective meaning to the proposition which affirms subjectively the diurnal rotation of the earth; but no proposition can, at any given time, signify objectively more than the known objective facts to which it refers at the time: all its capacity for further objective meaning is in our intellect. I suppose we are speculatively ignorant of this limitation in the objective signification of general propositions, though we know the limitation practically; and hence the interest we evince in physical experiments like the above at Paris. Our ignorance consists in not duly estimating the heterogeneous character of general propositions—not clearly discriminating that their generality is only an intellectual conception; and hence, when we would know what the "diurnal rotation of the earth" signifies objectively, we must not speculatively inquire what objective facts the proposition will intellectually fit, and assume that they exist objectively; but we must examine sensibly to discover, as in the above pendulous experiments at Paris, what objective things really exist that will conform to the proposition.

I deem the above rule of interpretation as important as any which can be given in relation to language, and it applies as intelligibly to every general proposition as to the "diurnal rotation of the earth." In the "Polynesian Researches," published some years since in London, the author, in speaking of some islands in the Pacific Ocean, says, "The tide is here very singular. If influenced at all by the moon, it is in a very small degree only. The height to which the water rises varies but a few inches during the whole year. Whatever be the age or situation of the moon, the water is lowest at six in the morning, and the same hour in the evening, and highest at noon and midnight." The writer seems embarrassed by the usual indiscrimination between the intellectually conceived general proposition in relation to the influence of the moon over tides, and objective physical facts. If the seas to which the writer alludes exhibit no sensible response to the intellectually conceived power of the moon, the defect is no wonder of objective nature, but an instance of inapplicability in an intellectual conception of man. The proposition which imputes tides to the attraction of the sun and moon means, objectively, not every objective occurrence and thing that we can speculatively see the proposition will fit, but it means, objectively, such objective things only as we can find sensibly to agree with the proposition. To know therefore, intellectually, that the sun and moon influence the tides—that the earth revolves daily on its axis, and annually around the sun—that the earth is round, etc., is to know certain general propositions which our intellect feels to be severally true subjectively; but if we would know what any one of the propositions means objectively, we must not employ our intellects to conceive what objective things the proposition will fit, but we must employ our senses to discover, sensibly, what objective things exist that can be covered by the proposition. I am aware that such an interpretation of general propositions will dispel much intellectual and verbal enchantment; but it will make our knowledge wholesome, masculine, and conformable to the realities of existence. I know, however, we delight rather to deem every proposition sensibly significant of every sensible fact that the proposition will intellectually fit, irrespective of whether such facts are sensibly perceptible or not. That the limitation is consequential which I thus speculatively assert, we may know; for when a person disregards the limitation, and deems himself revolving with the earth as physically as he may see a fly revolve with a revolving artificial globe, he feels an amazement that is not excited by any of the sensible perceptions which constitute the sensible meaning of the astronomical general propositions that impute revolutions to the earth.

§ 2. Every new proposition that the English language can make is only a new collocation of old words; just as a compositor sets in type different sentences by only changing the collocation of the same types. A complete permutation, like that imagined by Raymond Lully, of all the words in the English language, would exhibit every proposition that can be made in English; but many of the new propositions would be objectively insignificant till time should furnish some objects which the intellectual propositions would fit. We read in ancient history of "Greek fire;" but as we know not any objective things which the phrase intellectually fits, the phrase is objectively insignificant. When a schoolboy learns, intellectually, that every verb must agree with its nominative case in number and person, he may know none of the objective applications of the rule; and after a child has learned, intellectually, that twice one is two, he has still to learn the objective significations of the formula; as, for instance, that one apple and another are, objectively, equal to two apples. I mean not to say that a boy's intellect will never learn spontaneously that one apple and another are objectively equal to two apples; the intellects of men are so alike organically, that what one man's intellect conceives on any given occasion, another man's will be likely to conceive when similarly induced (just as what one man's arms will perform on some emergency, other men's will be likely to perform under a like emergency); but if to know, intellectually, that twice one is two, includes not necessarily the objective knowledge that one apple and another are two; no other general proposition that we may know intellectually will necessarily involve a knowledge of any of its objective meanings.

The general proposition attributed to Columbus, that he could make an egg stand on end is useful in at least showing the distinction between a general proposition and its objective meanings, and thereby disabusing us of the fallacious indiscrimination that is common in us between an intellectual knowledge of a general proposition and its sensible significations. In short, every general proposition possesses as many different objective meanings as it refers to different objects, and we must interpret every general proposition as we interpret, in an indictment, a general accusation of mutiny, treason, or felony. The general accusation is subjective, and refers to the intellect; but when we would know what the general accusation means objectively, we must examine the specifications for particular actions, and they alone can yield us unsophistically the answer.

No person can read Spurzheim's Treatise on Phrenology without discovering, intellectually, the connection which his intellect saw between our emotional and intellectual activity, etc., and certain protuberances of our brain and cranium; but the general propositions that his intellect conceived thereon can mean, objectively, no more than the limited number of objective facts that can be realized unverbally. Subject to the same objective limitation is the major proposition which makes the whole brain the organ of intelligence—a sort of *imperium in imperio*, or great natural galvanic battery; from which nerves, like galvanic wires, issue and ramify over all parts of the body, carrying to the brain communications from the external world by contact in the perceptions of touch—by pictures formed on the retina of the eye in the perception of sights—by appulses on the tympanum of the ear in the perception of sounds—by effluvia to the olfactory nerves in the perception of smells—and by papilla on the tongue in the perception of tastes. No general proposition is more subjectively satisfactory to the intellect than the foregoing in relation to the brain; still its objective, unverbal meaning must, like the objective, unverbal meaning of every other general proposition, be limited by the discoverable unverbal objects to which it refers.

§ 3. To limit the objective or unverbal signification of every proposition to the unverbal objects to which it refers, may seem to conflict with what in law is called circumstantial evidence. That Thomas struck the blow which killed John may be substantiated without proving the blow, but by showing that a cry of murder proceeded from a house out of which Thomas, covered with blood, was seen to issue; and that John, recently killed, was found alone in the house, with the sword of Thomas in his heart, etc. These objective facts include not any act of

Thomas which will be included by the proposition that he murdered John; still apparently they are all the objective facts on which a jury may find a verdict of wilful murder against him. Why, therefore, cannot certain sensible appearances, etc., in relation to the earth's diurnal revolution around its axis, prove not themselves only, but, in addition, other sensible facts not discoverable sensibly in the earth, but discoverable in the revolution of say an artificial sphere, etc.? The difference in the two cases may be stated as follows:—The objective facts which are manifested on the trial of Thomas, prove more than themselves by means of our objective experience with men like Thomas, their motives, actions, etc.; but the objective facts discoverable in the earth, etc., prove more than themselves, not by means of our objective experience with any thing like the earth, but with artificial spheres, etc., which we intellectually assume the earth to be like; so that really our theoretical conclusion of the earth's physical identicalness in revolution, with the revolution of an artificial sphere, partakes of the nature of a petitio principii. I must not, however, be understood as denying the revolution of the earth, as an intellectual proposition. I am only maintaining that the unverbal sensible meaning of the revolution is limited by the sensible facts which we can discover in relation thereto; and that all we superadd is subjective, not objective; intellectual, not physical. But I shall have occasion to speak further on such general propositions in our next lecture.

§ 4. Scientific general propositions such as we have been considering, possess determinate objective sensible meanings; but books and conversation are full of general propositions which partake more of the intellectual character of riddles than of specific objective communications. If a man has been thrown from the back of a vicious horse and wounded, he may relate the accident objectively in words like the above, or he may refer to it subjectively, in one or several enigmatical general propositions: as, "when we seek pleasure, we may find pain; what we employ as a substitute for medicine, may occasion a necessity for medicine; brute animals are so destitute of gratitude, that the more you pamper them with food, the more they will repay you with injury." He can construct as many such enigmatical general propositions as his intellect shall deem analogous to his accident; and they may all mean objectively, no more than the one accident. When you hear from him one of these propositions, the chance that you will interpret it objectively, by the accident, if it be unknown to you, is about equal to your chance of guessing what objective things I refer to when I say that I had a nice dish for my dinner to-day. Still your intellect will probably endeavour to find some objective physical meaning to his general proposition; and you will seek it among such of the objective things known to you as the general proposition will seem to fit. Should you succeed in finding any such objective thing, you will assent to the truth of his general proposition, "that brute animals are so destitute of gratitude, that the more you pamper them with food, the more they will repay you with ingratitude;" though perhaps all you mean is, that the more you feed your cat, the more neglectful she becomes of clearing your house from mice.

You may, however, recollect no objective thing which seems to accord with the above proposition, and by an antagonism to which the intellect is organically prone, you may be induced to recollect some objective things which contradict the proposition; as, for instance, the more you have housed and fed poultry during the winter, the more eggs they have furnished for your table; or the more you have provided appropriate food for your apiary, the more its bees have repaid you with honey. You will, therefore, deny his general proposition, and adduce these instances as proofs of its falsity. So a man who picked up a dollar which he saw fall from a traveller, went to a tavern, and in conversation with the landlord, made this general proposition: "Men are more honest in great matters than in small." He meant that he acted dishonestly in not restoring the dollar, whilst in his more extensive intercourse with mankind he was honest. The innkeeper, (who had a week previously found in one of his chambers a pocket-book with bank-notes, which he intended to keep, though he frequently corrected errors when his guests gave inadvertently some trifle too much,) replied, that he thought "men were more honest in small matters than in great."

"We are," says Professor Stewart, "enabled by our instinctive anticipations of physical events, to accommodate our conduct to what we perceive is to happen." This general proposition will be objectively insignificant to every person whose intellect cannot attach to it some objective incident which the intellect shall deem it to fit. The object of which it caused me to think, was the falling of a tree. Instinctive anticipation would enable me to perceive that I should be crushed if I did not change my position. Probably Professor Stewart thought of something different, and the fall of a tree may never have occurred to his observation. The inexperience of children tends to make general propositions objectively unintelligible to them; hence books intended for children, should avoid general propositions which are only intellectual vestments, and for which children may possess no sensible bodies.

§ 5. Other writers avoid the above enigmatical, objective unintelligibility. If they intellectually involve any objective fact in a general proposition, they subjoin the fact by way of sample, though it often constitutes all the objective meaning of their general proposition; thus, "the more," says St. Pierre, "temples are multiplied in a state, the more is religion enfeebled." What did St. Pierre mean? You will find in his succeeding paragraph:—"Look," says he, "at Italy covered with churches, yet Constantinople is crowded with Italian renegadoes; while the Jews, who had but one temple, are so strongly attached to their religion, that the loss of their temple excites to this day their regret." Mr. Hawkesbee asserts that the aurora borealis is the effect of electricity on a vacuum. What does he mean by his general proposition? He states subsequently as follows:—"The excitation of electricity in an exhausted Florence flask produced a light which resembled the aurora." Another person who shall find that all the phenomena of the aurora borealis cannot be thus imitated, will insist that Mr. Hawkesbee is wrong; but both are right intellectually, for they severally mean *objectively*, no more than the objects to which each refers. To speak thus of single physical facts as general propositions, enables us to seem physically rich on a very small actual capital; but without any determinate motive, the tendency of the intellect in every man, is strong to such subjective generalization; and like every organic tendency, it no doubt subserves useful purposes when judiciously employed.

To compel all men to employ the same collocation of words, is impracticable. The attempt has filled the world with controversy, and not brought us to the desired uniformity. I am so confident that nearly every general proposition is true, in the manner intended by the speaker, that I never contradict:—Cullen asserts, "that when an external cause produces in us a morbid action, Nature exerts an opposite process to counteract the evil." Some medical writers assert a conflicting general proposition. They say, "that every morbid change which occurs in our system is essentially injurious, and must be opposed by medicine." Two physicians who should severally enforce a different one of the above general propositions, supposing both propositions to refer to the same objective diseased condition, would employ opposite remedies. But to act thus proceeds from an erroneous belief that the general propositions are objectively significant of more than certain definite particulars. A person who knows the objective particulars to which the framer of each general proposition alludes, will probably find that both propositions are correct in the restricted cases.

Physicians have much employed such verbal controversy on the origin of yellow fever, some asserting as a general proposition that it is indigeneous, and others exotic. Were each partizan to detail the unverbal objective particulars to which his general proposition refers, no disagreement would probably exist; but while he deems his general proposition significant objectively of more than certain unverbal particulars, endless verbal controversy ensues. Each thinks justly that the other errs, for the same mistake of the nature of general propositions misleads both. A father said once, "My son, in water exists a principle which is destructive of life; and in brandy, a principle preservative of life." The father meant objectively, that total immersion in water would produce death, and that a small quantity of brandy was occasionally salutary. The proposition was correct while confined to the objects to which the father alluded; but the son, supposing its application as universal unverbally, as verbally, refrained from the use of water, and substituted brandy. We all err, though not always in a like degree, when we consider any general proposition significant objectively of more than certain objective particulars; and if those who promulge general propositions will not announce the objective particulars to which they refer, the proposition is to us only a sort of intellectual garment with which we may invest any unverbal object that our intellect shall happen to know, and deem the proposition to fit; but the proposition will not necessarily teach us the objective meaning referred to by the promulgers of the proposition. Speculative writers are particularly fruitful of general propositions, and usually without subjoining any objective example by way of key to the respective riddles which they thus construct. Books, however, of every kind, abound with unexplained general propositions,—to frame general propositions being much less laborious than to furnish them with substantial objective bodies. Politicians find such propositions a convenient mode of expressing opinions that will suit everybody; for instance, "a judicious tariff" is precisely what every man desires, though one man may mean thereby an import duty of a hundred per cent. ad valorem, and another man may mean a total exemption from any duty. "To demand from foreign nations nothing but what ought to be demanded, and to submit to nothing but what ought to be submitted to," is a proposition which will meet with universal assent, though conduct entirely opposite in character may be covered thereby. "To give to every private individual the utmost personal liberty that is useful to the individual himself as well as to the nation," will meet the approbation of the most liberal democrat and the most tyrannical autocrat. All such propositions are like the bathing dresses supplied to visitors on the beach at Newport; they fit everybody equally well, but the bodies clothed thereby exhibit, when uncovered, every sort of variety that bodies are capable of assuming. Silence has been long denoted a characteristic of wisdom; and when we consider the character of general propositions, we see a propriety in refraining from speech if we have nothing to communicate but general propositions; though the difficulty in acquiring sensible facts deserving of specific announcement, must impose much silence on any man who should employ them as his only topics of conversation. The scarcity in which new sensible facts exist, is usually illustrated very painfully when scientific men meet together formally, in public associations, to interchange information. What a relief on such an emergency is some narrative like the late soundings of the ocean by Lieutenant Maury, which speaks of something besides ever changing, ever conflicting intellectually conceived opinions. The specific sensible facts that are usually announced at such meetings compare in number with the general propositions in about the relation of a grain of wheat to a peck of chaff.

§ 6. Before I close the present Lecture, I want to make a few remarks on propositions which possess little or no objective signification, and whose signification is mostly or wholly subjective. Such propositions are easily constructed, and books of every description abound with them. The intellect discovers in the words a syntactical congruity to each other; hence the propositions possess a hazy intellectual intelligence, which satisfies the author and often pleases the feelings of the reader. "Fellow citizens!" might a Fourth of July orator say, in accordance with the above species of propositions—"the destiny of our beloved country is in our keeping, let us be faithful to our sacred trust, and support no man for any public station who will not advocate principles that will bear the scrutiny of virtue; for, without virtue, all seeming prosperity is baseless, and all seeming good but evil in disguise. Oh! that this important truth could be wafted by the four winds of heaven, and impressed, as with the point of a diamond, on the hearts of the rising generation; then, indeed, would our teeming population, from the wide Atlantic to the broad Pacific, become a great and glorious nation, for we should be a virtuous people. Finally, fellow citizens, let us not be deceived by false demagogues who speak what they mean not, but let us believe honest patriots who mean what they speak, though they tell us unpalatable truths."

Propositions like the above assimilate to poetry or music. They speak to the feelings rather than to the intellect, and hence probably their power to please. The feelings can be affected irrespective wholly of the objective meaning of words, as we find in very young children, to whom the songs which induce tranquillity or pleasure can communicate no objective information. Nor ought we to deem propositions, such as the foregoing oration, destitute of utility when addressed to men. I once went with a gentleman to an oratorio, where, after a few intellectually unintelligible words had been sung, and repeated often in melodious tones and with melodious accompaniments, he observed to me, that he had derived from what he had heard, more religious feelings than he had ever obtained from intellectual sermons. So, probably, a Fourth of July oration, which communicates no objective information, may yet promote the patriotic feelings of the hearers, or cultivate in them other beneficial feelings, and thus influence their conduct more beneficially than any number of precepts with any amount of objective signification. Indeed, no inconsiderable part of all prayers and sermons derive their cogency from their effect on our internal feelings; hence, when listened to for objective information, the listeners constitute usually the most dissatisfied portion of the audience. The organic principle, by which words are thus efficacious over our internal feelings, has not received the speculative consideration that the principle merits. I have presented my views thereon in Lecture V. of a small book, entitled "Religion in its Relation to the present Life," published for me, in 1841, by Harper & Brothers, of New York, and to which I refer because any direct consideration of the subject would not be within the proper purview of the present work.

§ 7. Having thus shown, I hope sufficiently, that the objective signification of every general proposition is only the objective particulars to which the proposition refers, and that no verbal universality of the purview of any proposition can make it significant unverbally beyond the above limits, I might dismiss the subject, except that a verbal puzzle is connected with the assigned limits. A man, for instance, who lives within the tropics, may never have heard that light and darkness are not diurnally successive in every part of the earth; and no general proposition will be more incontestible to his intellect than the diurnal alternation, *everywhere*, of light and darkness. We know, however, that the man is mistaken; and why may we not be mistaken in our belief that every unsupported stone will everywhere fall towards the earth, and that every man will die? The question I will reserve for our next Lecture, as it involves an important principle in the interpretation of general propositions, and otherwise deserves a separate consideration.

LECTURE VII.

OF THE UNFALLACIOUS MEANING OF NEGATIVE GENERAL PROPOSITIONS.

CONTENTS.

A negation that refers to no physical object, is physically insignificant.
An affirmation that is universal in its terms, and unlimited by any sensible negative, is still significant sensibly of only the sensible objects to which it refers.

§ 1. As no proposition can signify, objectively, more than the objects to which it refers, every proposition in the form of a negation is necessarily unmeaning, objectively, when it refers to no objective thing. The limitation is not conventional, but pertains to language constitutionally: when, therefore, a man within the tropics asserts that light and darkness alternate diurnally *everywhere*, he is correct to the extent only of the physical particulars to which he refers; but a negation of his proposition is also significant physically, because the negation refers to physical facts that occur beyond the tropics. If, however, I assert that unsupported stones may, in some unexplored part of the earth, not fall towards the earth, I shall refer to no physical fact, and hence my salvo will be physically insignificant.

The limitation above stated, in the unverbal meaning of negative propositions, possesses great practical importance, and has, I suppose, not received the speculative recognition which it merits. I solicit for it, therefore, much attention, and will give some further examples of my meaning: —An Esquimaux Indian will be as positive that water everywhere freezes during the winter, as I am that a piece of gold will everywhere exhibit the sight round, and the feel round, when the piece is so formed that a line drawn from the centre of it to the surface, anywhere, will measure just one inch. Now I know that the Esquimaux is mistaken. Countries exist in which water never freezes, and why may not countries exist in which physical objects are so different from those with which I am acquainted, that a piece of gold may possess the proportions that I have stated, and still not be round? The two propositions are verbally alike, but unverbally different. That countries exist in which water never freezes is significant unverbally, for the affirmation refers to the sensible experience of credible witnesses; but the doubt in relation to the gold is merely verbal, or, at most, intellectual. It refers to no sensible experience, and hence is as sensibly insignificant as any story of fairies that amuses infancy, and for precisely the same reason, and for no other reason.

That the dead exhibit neither sensation nor consciousness is nearly all we mean objectively when we assert that the dead are void of feeling and consciousness. We cannot know, experimentally, that the dead suffer no pain on a funeral pyre, or under the knife of an anatomical demonstrator, or under the process of decomposition. You may deem this intellectual reflection full of horror, and deprecate for the dead some attention to the intellectually alleged possibility of their latent sensibilities. But you will deprecate in vain. The anatomical demonstrator will proceed in his dissecting operations as unconcernedly as before. He may not be able to state why he practically disregards your remarks; but the reason lies in his practical acquaintance with the nature of language. Your remarks refer to nothing sensible, hence he knows them to be sensibly insignificant. No views of language manifest so well the secret of its significancy as the contemplation of salvos like the foregoing. The contingencies are objectively insignificant from no lack of subjective significancy, but simply because they possess no objective meaning. They are intellectual garments which ostensibly are capable of fitting somebody, but no physical body is adapted to them. They are worse than the slipper of Cinderella, for one foot was found that it could fit; but a reservation which refers to no unverbal object, is objectively meaningless.

§ 2. We may apply remarks like the foregoing to numerous scientific propositions. For instance, the intellect of every man conceives irresistibly, from existing premises, that the earth is round, and that it is subject to diurnal and annual motions; but should a man assert that the roundness and motions thus conceived of the earth are not associated with any physical roundness and motions, his negation will be physically significant to only the extent of the sensible perceptions to which it refers; and when any such negation refers to nothing that is sensibly perceptible, the negation will be sensibly insignificant. These doctrines may be thought to conflict with what I have said heretofore on such propositions, and I contrast the two doctrines the better to explain them. My former comments on such doctrines, in their affirmative announcement, were directed not against the propriety of the announcement, but against imputing to the propositions a physical meaning beyond the sensible particulars on which the doctrines are founded. I suppose I am not mistaken in believing that men are accustomed to deem the affirmative diurnal and annual motions conceived of the earth, etc., not limited insensible signification to the sensible particulars to which the intellectually conceived motions relate; we include therewith and confound as sensible much that is only intellectually conceived. And here again you may ask me what is the difference between what is only intellectually conceived and what can be sensibly perceived; and I again answer, that it is what it is; the difference is unverbal, not verbal, and words can only refer us to it. Unverbal things cannot be transmuted into words, or vice versâ; and if no unverbal difference exists between what is only intellectually conceived and what is sensibly perceived, my whole speculative superstructure is inane—a distinction without a difference; though our bias towards confounding the two, or rather the piquancy which attends the materializing of what we conceive intellectually, is conclusive to, at least, my feelings, that an unverbal and consequential difference exists between what we intellectually conceive and what we sensibly perceive.

Similar to the foregoing are the intellectually conceived assertions, that the moon and the sun cause the tides; that every fixed star is a sun, and the centre of a planetary system; that beyond all telescopic vision other stars exist, which also are the centres of more remote systems; that the earth appears like a star to the inhabitants of the planets, etc. Now, if a person chooses to say that no physical realities exist that conform to these intellectual conceptions, his negation will possess no physical significance beyond the sensible perceptions to which his negation may refer, and the negation will be wholly insignificant sensibly if it refer to nothing sensible. The absence of a physical negative will make any affirmative proposition true universally; yet the universal affirmation will still mean, physically, the physical particulars only to which the affirmation refers. A nursery couplet says, "The children of Holland take pleasure in making, what the children of England take pleasure in breaking." I want to avoid a like conduct if possible, though it is quite prevalent in speculative controversy. I take no pleasure in subverting any received speculative tenets, and only endeavour to manifest their proper unverbal signification.

And now a friend suggests to me the following queries: —"Have you any objective reasons for disbelieving that the earth would appear like a star, if you could view it from any of the planets which belong to our solar system? —have you any objective reasons for disbelieving it would exhibit the sight round and the feel round, if you could possibly see it and feel it in entirety, as you can see and feel an artificial globe?—have you any objective reasons for disbelieving that the earth's motions would be as sensibly perceptible as an artificial globe's, were you located in relation to the earth as you are located in relation to an artificial globe?" To these queries I answer, that as they refer to nothing sensible that is within my knowledge, they are to me sensibly insignificant; but my intellect sees the cogency of the questions, and cannot avoid assenting thereto; and the intellectual assent no way conflicts with any position I have intended to establish. If any person shall discover a verbal conflict, the discovery will arise from my inability to express verbally what I intended unverbally.

I have treated far too summarily the important truths which the present Lecture embraces within its proper purview, but I will close it with an illustration of the embarrassment we may experience when we know not that a negation is subject to the same limitation in its unverbal interpretation as an affirmation; namely, that neither can mean objectively more than the objects to which it refers; and that either is insignificant sensibly when it refers to no sensible object. I once heard a celebrated clergyman astonish and puzzle his hearers by the announcement that experience alone would not authorize the belief that we must all die; experience being able, he said, to speak of the past only—not of the future. He insisted that we can be affirmatively certain of death from only its being a prediction of revelation. Now the puzzle of the above vanishes when we discriminate between its intellectual significancy and its sensible significancy. That we must all die refers, certainly for its sensible signification, to only our sensible experience; but any doubt in relation thereto, and any negative in relation thereto, refer to no sensible experience, and, consequently, both doubt and negative are sensibly insignificant.

LECTURE VIII.

OF THE UNFALLACIOUS INTERPRETATION OF WORDS THAT ARE INTELLECTUALLY CONCEIVED.

CONTENTS.

1. Words conceived by the intellect mean, unverbally, the organism of the intellect; not the objects which the words mean when they apply to the perceptions of the senses.
2. Intellectually conceived words are subjective responses of the intellect to objective premises.
3. As a man increases his objective knowledge, he increases the material out of which his intellect conceives its subjective responses.
4. The intellect cannot originate objective knowledge except what relates to its own organism.
5. The responses of the intellect are independent of our volition.

§ 1. We are now arrived where we may usefully reflect upon so much of what we have accomplished as is necessary to make the past subsidiary to the future. The unverbal meaning of words is our theme; what the unverbal meanings are is the object of our researches. To make words tell what unverbal meanings are has always led speculation to where it wanders "in endless mazes lost;" and the result, as well as the attempt, may be likened to the efforts of a child to outrun its shadow, or of a kitten, by revolving, to catch its own tail. Words are as unable to tell us what unverbal things are as the sounds of a bell are unable to tell us what unsonorous things are; or, as visible appearances, pictures, etc., are unable to tell us what invisible things are; or, as odours are unable to tell us what inodorous things are. What unverbal things are we can be told by only the mute unverbal revelations of our senses, internal feelings, and intellect. Into these alone we must translate words when we desire to know the ultimate unverbal signification of the words; and this mode of interpreting words constitutes one of the main precepts that I have attempted to inculcate.

§ 2. Unverbal things which I have thus postulated as the ultimate signification of words, differ among themselves generically; the revelations of each of our five senses differing from the revelations of the other four; and the revelations of the intellect and of the internal feelings differing from each other, and from sensible perceptions. Our speculative disregard of the generic differences which thus exist in our sensible, moral, and intellectual knowledge, (our estimating unverbal things by their verbal homogeneity rather than by their unverbal heterogeneity,) must, at some future period of the world's existence, astonish our successors, as much as we are astonished that our predecessors could ever believe that the intellectually conceived flight through the air of witches on broomsticks was homogeneous with a visible flight through the air of birds. When a juggler opens a box, and shows us it is empty, and again opens it and we find it full of sand, and again opens it and we see it full of live birds; we are surprised, for we have not seen that the box possesses three different compartments. We employ words with the same delusive misunderstanding. The word revolution, for instance, refers unverbally in one use of it, to the sensible (visible and tactile) revolution of a cart-wheel or a boy's top; and in another use of it to the intellectually conceived relation which men personally bear to the earth in its intellectually conceived revolutions around its axis and around the sun; but when we suppose that in both uses (the revolutions intellectually imputed to us personally and to the earth, and the revolution sensibly imputed to the cart-wheel and the top,) the word revolution possesses a meaning that is homogeneous, we are as much surprised at the verbal equivoke, which deems us and the earth thus to revolve, as we are at the juggle of the conjurer; and the source of the surprise is alike fallacious in both cases. To estimate unverbal things by their generic differences, despite their verbal homogeneity, as in the above examples, has been another of the purposes which I have endeavoured to accomplish; and after a short familiarity with the generic discrimination in the unverbal signification of words, every man will be delighted with the clearness which it will confer on his knowledge, and the immunity it will yield him from mysteries.

Colloquial language has been unpremeditatedly fashioned by our practical knowledge of the above generic differences that we speculatively disregard. We talk, for instance, of our ability or inability, as the case may be, to *feel* the truth of a given remark—to *feel* ashamed, excited, elated, proud, humble, envious, jealous, etc.; thus denoting that the words designate severally an internal *feeling*. We talk of an ability or inability, as the case may be, to *conceive* how the soul is united to the body; how the dead are to appear bodily in another world; how effects are united to causes, etc.; thus denoting that the words designate severally intellectual conceptions, not sensible perceptions. We talk of *hearing* thunder, *seeing* lightning, *perceiving* or smelling odours, *feeling* cold, etc.; thus denoting that the words designate sensible perceptions, and of different senses. The litany of the Episcopal church prays for deliverance from temptations of "the world, the flesh, and the devil;" which expressions recognise, as I suppose, the three generically different departments of our unverbal knowledge—the "world" designating sensible temptations; the "flesh" designating temptations of the internal feelings; and the "devil" designating temptations from intellectual suggestions. The Bible, in many places, triplicates thus its allusions to our triple organism; and often, though not always, employs the word flesh as in the above example:—"the spirit is willing, but the flesh is weak"; the spirit denotes the intellect; the flesh, the feelings. A volume might be written of such biblical generic discriminations, and profitably written, I think, to familiarise us with the unverbal triplicity of man's nominal oneness.

§ 3. The foregoing are all that I will recapitulate of

what I have yet accomplished, if I may hope a full fruition of what I have attempted. But now arises the most pregnant and subtile difficulty that is connected with my speculations, or with speculations generally. I alluded to it in my introductory lecture, and said I should speak more on the subject thereafter; and I am now to fulfil that promise. The five senses yield unverbal utterances, sights, sounds, tastes, feels, smells, which every person can understand unverbally. The utterance of each sense is known also to be peculiar; and we can readily translate into such unverbal sensible utterances, any word that relates to sensible revelations. The internal feelings also possess unverbal emotional utterances, and into the unverbal emotions we can readily translate anger, and every other word that relates to any internal feeling; but the intellect conceives in *words,* and thus the intellect seems to possess no *unverbal* utterances. A very important question therefore arises, whether our intellectually conceived words possess any unverbal meaning—any meaning ulterior to the conceived words. I, at one period, supposed they possess no ulterior meaning, and that all abstract speculations are mere words. Twice one house is two houses, and twice one fairy is two fairies. The first proposition is significant of more than words, because it refers to something unverbal; but the second is mere words, I said, because it refers to nothing that is unverbal. I should probably have continued in this short-sighted belief, had I not found that a vast amount of human learning, including all natural theology, is involved in the issue; and perhaps all revealed theology. When, for instance, I look at the sun, my intellect will irresistibly conceive that its existence had a commencement, that its origin needed a maker, that it is a design of some designer, a contrivance of some contriver, an effect of some cause; hence, as affirmed by natural theology, any intellect will be forced onward and upwards to the conception in words of a first cause, a first contriver, designer and maker, who is himself uncaused, uncontrived, undesigned, uncreated. Indeed, all the fundamental tenets of theology, with an after-life retribution of bliss or woe, have been conceived (variously modified) by all men in all ages; so that to doubt whether such conceptions belong to the human intellect is as irrational, as to doubt whether walking, seeing, tasting, feeling, hope, fear, and hunger, belong to our sensible and moral nature.

§ 4. To find that such verbal conceptions are indigenous to the human intellect, not foreign grafts thereon by priestcraft, as some suppose, is one step gained in the direction of right knowledge, and probably the most important step; but are such intellectual conceptions verbal only, or possess the conceived words a meaning that is unverbal? We can look behind words that relate to sensible perceptions and internal feelings, and find objects that are unverbal; but can we look behind intellectually conceived words and find anything unverbal? Revelation, I think, answers the question; and though I mean not to found my doctrine thereon, but contrariwise the interpretation is founded on my doctrine; yet I deem the coincidence valuable and remarkable:—St. Luke "was demanded of the Pharisees when the kingdom of God should come;" and he answered them and said, "the kingdom of God is *within you;*" which signifies, as I suppose, that "the kingdom of God" are intellectually conceived words whose unverbal meaning is subjective, not objective; in our intellect, and not anything physical, though we seem to suppose the meaning to be physical, when we point our finger upwards when we speak of the kingdom of God; and point our finger downwards, when we speak of the kingdom of Satan; whose meaning also is within us.

But what is *in us* besides the conceived *words?* that is the question which I am to consider. The organism is within us, from which the conceived words proceed. A man's imprecations of curses on his eyes, body and soul, are words; but they are also signs of an unverbal internal feeling *in* the organism of the imprecator:—So "the kingdom of God" are words, but the words are also signs of an unverbal impulse or tendency in the organism of our intellect; as, therefore, the internal organic feeling which prompts an imprecation is the unverbal meaning of the imprecation; so the organism of the intellect that conceives any given words is the unverbal meaning of the verbal conception.

Many commentators interpret the text of St. Luke as referring to the internal feelings which predominate in devout Christians, and "the kingdom of God" may doubtless be in a man unverbally *in both ways;* but in both ways the *unverbal* meaning is alike subjective, not objective; in one case the unverbal meaning is in the organism of the feelings, and in the other in the organism of the intellect; and in both cases the organisms are part of every man's nature, hence the conceived words possess an unverbal meaning as truly as the words horse or orange. Remember that our disquisitions relate to only the unverbal meaning of *words,* or rather of sounds, (which all words are,) in themselves as unmeaning as the bellow of a bull or the crow of a cock; and as little intelligible, except in the country whose people have converted the given sounds into words, by attaching to the sounds something that is unverbal; a something that must have reference to the organism of the speakers, for we can no more invent a word whose unverbal meaning can surpass the purview of our organisms, than we can invent a new sense.

§ 5. In further corroboration that the above interpretation of the unverbal meaning of intellectually conceived words is not repugnant to the Scriptures, revelation continually warns us against affixing an objective meaning to such of its tenets as the intellect can conceive in words only. A remarkable warning of this kind, in relation to Deity, is contained in the second commandment of the Decalogue. The intellect alone can conceive Deity unphysically, but the intellect can manifest the conception only by words; and such words will be vox et preterea nihil, unless we find for them an *unverbal* meaning in the intellectual organism from which the conceived words proceed. Indeed, revelation characterizes as mysteries, all of its tenets that like omniscience, omnipotence, trinity in unity, etc., are, objectively, only intellectually conceived words; and towards them, nothing is required of us but faith, which is an internal *feeling* that we know, experimentally, the intellectual conceptions are capable of exciting.

I will add in further illustration of the above interpretation of intellectually conceived words, and not to make innovations in theology, that St. John says, "In the beginning was the Word, and the Word was with God, and the Word *was* God." Now I suppose the text to affirm that our meaning of God, apart from the word God, was only subjective; till, as St. John says, subsequently, "The Word was made flesh and dwelt among us," and thereby gave the word God an objective meaning.

Let us present another illustration of the unverbal meaning of intellectually conceived *words:* the intellect insists on conceiving that what we see, feel, taste, hear, and smell, are not physical copies of any external things, but only subjective *effects* produced on our senses by some external objective "*substance*," which we are incapable of knowing sensibly except by the sensible effects on us it thus produces. This doctrine philosophers deem entirely satisfactory. But the conceived "substance," which is thus knowable only verbally by the intellect, bears the same subjective relation to the intellect that conceives it as sensible qualities bear to the senses; the intellectually conceived verbal "substance" being an effect only of our intellectual organism, as sensible qualities are effects only of our sensible organs. What then is ultimate to the verbal "substance" which the intellect thus conceives? The organism of our intellect, of which the verbal conception is an effect; and we can know no more in relation thereto. Our verbal conceptions of Deity, and of every kindred truth, are like the above verbally conceived "substance;" they belong to the nature of our intellect, and are, *unverbally*, part of every man's ego. The intellect organically craves to know more in relation to its conceptions, and may conceive thereon more *words;* but all such words will only be further effects of the organism of the intellect, and that organism will constitute the ultimate meaning of the conceived words, proceed with such conceptions as far as our dictionaries and other vocabularies will supply words.

§ 6. When we deem intellectually conceived words a manifestation of the organism of our intellect, as just stated, we obtain the most satisfactory understanding of them that we are capable of obtaining. Instead, however, of being satisfied with this subjective meaning, we often seek an objective meaning; and from an inability of finding any objective meaning, many intellectually conceived words are deemed insignificant. Men, thus influenced, scoff at the words spirit, immateriality, immortality, resurrection, heaven, hell, etc.; but, properly understood, the words denote an organism of the intellect, or the intellect could not habitually, in all ages of the world and in all places form such conceptions. I have drawn most of my illustrations of this tenet of my doctrines from subjects connected with theology, not because intellectually conceived words on theology differ essentially from other verbal conceptions of the intellect, but because literature is full of splendid wrecks, in proof that no teachings can be useful or durable unless they are reconcileable with revelation. All intellectually conceived words, whether relating to sacred subjects or profane, must alike find their ultimate unverbal meaning in the organism of the intellect; just as all sounds produced by a piano must rest ultimately on the organism of the piano; and as all sensible perceptions must rest ultimately on the organism of our senses; and as all we eat must depend for its effects on the organism of our stomach.

The tenets of geology, that anticipate sensible researches in relation to the stratification of the earth, etc., my intellect recognizes as consonant to its organism; hence, my intellect assents to them; and my intellect conceives just as necessarily that the earth is the product of some maker; that its existence had a commencement, and will have a termination; but if I fail to see that these intellectual conceptions are all subjective knowledge, not objective, I have yet to learn the correct unverbal interpretation of intellectually conceived words. Vitality, gravitation, wisdom, electricity, etc., are also words that the intellect is organized to conceive; but not otherwise than it is organized to conceive the words soul, Deity, conscience, heaven, hell, immortality, resurrection, etc.; hence we discover how vain are all hopes or fears in relation to the permanence of religion. It possesses an unverbal subjective reality, which is as organic, and hence as little dependent for its permanence on fashion and caprice, as hunger, hope, fear, or the perception of colours and figures.

When we deem religion a human contrivance—a device of priestcraft—two essentially different things are confounded; namely, forms of worship and verbal creeds are confounded with the intellectual and moral organisms from which creeds and forms originate. Creeds and forms are only an *objective* verbal manifestation of a *subjective* unverbal impulse or state of the intellect and feelings. Creeds and forms of worship have changed repeatedly, and are changing continually; but the intellectual organism from which creeds and forms of worship proceed, must insure the perpetuity of creeds in some form; and our internal feelings are so organized, that the feelings which give unction to present creeds and forms, and which formerly made sacred the nominal units Jupiter and Pluto, must continue to give unction to any future creeds and forms that the intellect may conceive in substitution of the present; if we may, for illustration, conceive a radical change practicable, after our nearly two thousand years' experience to the contrary, and after attempts thereto by men of the most celebrated intellects. The ultimate results, therefore, which infidelity in existing creeds and forms can ever permanently accomplish, is the substitution of some new creeds and forms for those which exist at the time of the substitution.

As different men groan and imprecate differently, under the influence of the same internal feeling, so different men may conceive different verbal creeds, etc, under the influence of the same intellectual impulse; but the intellectual organic impulses of all men are probably alike *unverbally*, just as the internal feelings of all men are probably alike unverbally. When, however, we would look for a meaning behind the words which the intellect conceives on any such occasion, we can find nothing *unverbal* but the organism of the intellect; just as we can find nothing behind sensible perceptions but the organism of the senses. All beyond the purview of our three (sensible, intellectual, and moral) organisms is a terra incognita, which revelation doubtless alludes to, but which we can understand *objectively* no better than the blind can understand colours, or the deaf sounds; and even such a verbally conceived terra incognita is also, unverbally, only a result of our intellectual organism; and so is the further verbal conception, that the organization which relates to religious conceptions would not have been given to us were it not to be hereafter objectively realized.

§ 7. But while I am striving to discriminate, generically, intellectually conceived *words* from sensibly perceived *objects*, etc., I desire not to be understood as deeming intellectually conceived words inferior to sensible objects in dignity, purport, and character. We possess three generically different organisms—the intellect, the senses, and the internal feelings. Every man's verbal ego is thus essentially triune unverbally; and while every thing we can know must be subjective to one of these three sets of organs, no extra limitary criterion exists beyond the said organs by which we can decide which set of organs is most authoritative, or most entitled to our respect. Each is ultimate within its own sphere, and around each "a great gulf is fixed," which will not permit any one of the three sets of organs to invade *unverbally* the province of either of the other sets. We, however, continually employ the intellect to yield us physical information where our senses cease their purview. We desire to know what exists in the centre of the earth—when came it there—how, and whence; and to look forward into the undeveloped future, and backward down the unrecorded and even antediluvian past. But though the intellect will in such cases seem to yield us physical responses, yet the responsive words, in all such speculations, possess no unverbal meaning but what is subjective to the intellect that conceives them. The words will reflexly exhibit, to every man that conceives them, the organism of his intellect—its aspirations, its impulses, its conceptions; and they constitute to him the only unsophistical unverbal meaning of his intellectually conceived words in the cases above described. I censure no such use of our intellect, for the use is as inevitable and organic as any other, and the results are irresistibly operative on our internal feelings; hence, intellectually conceived words, in even the above cases, and in all cases, influence our conduct, and constitute as substantive a part of our knowledge as sensible information, though of a different generic character. In short, when a man has analyzed his intellectually conceived words into what is unverbal in relation thereto, he is at the end of his unverbal knowledge in the premises; and if we say of such intellections as possess no sensible reference, that they are what they are, we shall speak of them more unsophistically than by characterizing them verbally in any other way; the ultimate elements of our knowledge being not words but unverbal things. The intellect strives to end every discussion with *words*—it organically struggles for the last word; but the end of every disquisition must be *unverbal*, if we would obtain an end that is unsophistical.

§ 8. I much suspect that deeming all intellectually conceived words objective in their signification, makes us underestimate the intelligence of deaf mutes. We mistake in the mutes an absence of intellectually conceived words, for an absence of the intellectual unverbal impulses, etc., from which verbal conceptions proceed. The intellect of a deaf mute will, of course, not know that "the whole is greater than a part," but he will possess the unverbal intellectual impulse from which the verbal axiom originates; and he will resist as pertinaciously any subtraction from his possessions, as we whose intellect can conceive the maxim in words. His intellect will not conceive that "things equal to the same, are equal to each other;" yet he will possess the unverbal intellection which alone gives the axiom its intellectual signification; and he will evince that his unverbal intellection or impulse, is as influential over his physical conduct, as the axiom is over yours who can conceive the axiomatic words. His intellect will not conceive that "everything requires a maker;" that "everything is the effect of some cause," and that "every existence had a beginning, and must have a termination;" yet we can know from his general physical conduct, that he possesses the intellectual impulses which constitute the unverbal meaning of even such intellectually conceived words. Creeds he will, of course, not know; but the intellectual impulse or tendency which is unverbal in creeds, and which constitutes their unverbal cogency, unction and signification, he may know as well as we. Dickens' "Household Words" contains an article on idiots, as he saw them "at the Essex Hall Asylum for idiots, near Colchester," and the article countenances a belief that even idiots, who usually, in addition to their other intellectual defects, know no language, may possess measurably the unverbal impulses which constitute the subjective meaning of intellectually conceived words that possess no sensible meaning. He says the idiots "are very fond of attending prayers in a body. What dim religious impressions they connect with public worship it is impossible to say; but the struggling soul would seem to have some instinctive aspirations towards its Maker."

§ 9. I will now assume that all intellectually conceived

words possess a meaning which is unverbal. In view of the vast significance of the tenet, I feel that I have not manifested it as fully as it deserves; but if I have succeeded in making my meaning intelligible, I have accomplished all that I have contemplated in relation to the unverbal meaning of intellectually conceived words. Indeed, I only say enough on any topic to merit the character of suggestions; the full development of the topics—knowledge being progressive—I confidently expect, in the course of time, from men who may succeed me. My efforts must be considered as mere inklings of a new analysis of language, attempted in the briefest manner compatible with an exposition of my design. I have opened a mine which contains much precious metal, but what I exhibit are only rude specimens of the ore.

I will close this Lecture with a few collateral suggestions on the formation and nature of theories. The words which the intellect of any man conceives as a theory on any occasion are responses of his intellect to given premises; and the words that constitute every such theoretical response are as independent of the man's volition, as the pulsations of his heart, or the processes of his digestive organs. Were the responses not thus involuntary, the intellect would be like an oracle that could speak only what the interrogator should direct; and hence be useless. But while the theoretical responses of the intellect are involuntary, every verbal response of a man's intellect is derived from his objective knowledge; the intellect, in conceiving words, being like a man who is playing whist, and who can play such cards only as happen to have been dealt to him. We accordingly find that the intellect, in conceiving theories, conceives French words on one side of the British Channel, and English words on the other side; and in a rude age conceives rude theories, and in a refined age conceives subtile theories. A man's objective employments also regulate to a great degree the words that his intellect will conceive in its theoretical responses to given premises:—a chemist's intellect responding with words which relate to chemistry; a mechanic's, with words that relate to mechanics; and a mathematician's, with words that relate to mathematics, etc. Still, while the intellects of different men vary thus in the words which they conceive as theories on any given occasion, the intellectual organism that gives an unverbal meaning to the conceived words, may be much alike in all men, whatever difference exists being in quality rather than in kind; just as the physical actions of different men vary in modes of performance rather than in variety of actions; and just as an Esquimaux Indian and a London alderman differ in the food which they eat, while the organic impulse which craves food, and for which the food is eaten, is alike in both the persons. Hence, though the gravitation which the intellect conceives now as upholding the earth, is different, verbally, from the Atlantean shoulders that the intellect conceived formerly as upholding it; yet, except in differences that are sensibly perceptible, the two verbal theories signify unverbally only the organism of the intellect. We may repeat the same remark of all theories. "The horror of a vacuum," and "the pressure of the atmosphere," differ not from each other in the relation of truth and fiction; the modern theory may be more useful than the old, and its sensible meaning may refer to a greater number of sensibly perceptible particulars; but so much of both theories as is not sensibly perceptible, but only intellectually conceived, is subjective, and signifies, unverbally, nothing but the organism of the intellect—both the theories referring probably to the same organic unverbal impulse.

§ 10. As a consequence of the circumscription which thus seems to pertain to men's intellectual conceptions, the intellect is continually superseding old theories with new, as it acquires new objective knowledge. When earthquakes were felt in a rude age, the intellect of the observers responded thereto by conceiving, verbally, that imprisoned Titans were struggling to liberate themselves; but the discovery of gunpowder enabled the intellect to conceive that earthquakes were caused by spontaneously generated and spontaneously ignited gunpowder. On the discovery of steam power, the intellect was enabled to again amend its verbal theory by substituting steam as the conceived cause of earthquakes, and new verbal causes will continue to be conceived therefor to the end of time, as the intellect shall become acquainted with new objective agencies; the agency whose results the intellect shall deem most analogous to earthquakes, will always be the cause therefor which the intellect will verbally assign.

But I desire particularly to remark in relation to theories—and I solicit for the remark much attention—that every theory is a fiction to the extent that we employ it to materialize a modus operandi that is only intellectually conceived, and such a materialization is the object of every theory. The object is in its nature a fallacy, and unattainable; the intellect being organically incapable of revealing to us new physical existences: for instance, when I see a needle rush towards a magnet, my intellect is not satisfied with merely the sensible facts; it will organically insist on conceiving some physical modus operandi which shall assimilate what I see in the needle and magnet to what I experience in myself when I draw towards me a chair or some other object. To satisfy this organic impulse, the intellect will conceive some physical emanation from the magnet to the needle, or some other theoretical physical machinery; but the attempt becomes a delusion the moment we deem physical the intellectually conceived verbal theory. If a philosopher were to tell me that by means of a powerful microscope, he had become able to see the emanation from the magnet to the needle, I should know the statement was like the moon hoax, heretofore alluded to, and that he was labouring under some delusion. The emanation is only a conception of the intellect, and cannot be transmuted into a sensible reality, the two things being generically different, heterogeneous, and inconvertible. On this principle, I entertain no doubt that some fallacy exists in relation to the late pendulous experiments at Paris, and which seem to materialize unverbally the intellectually conceived diurnal motion of the earth—a conception as little likely to be realized physically as the once intellectually conceived residence of the soul in the pineal gland is likely to be realized physically; or as the intellectual conception of spectres, ghosts, fairies, and kindred beings, is likely to be realized physically. I shall not be surprised if, eventually, we discover also that some fallacy exists in the experiment of Dr. Maskelyn, in Perthshire, that a mountain will so attract a plummet as to prevent the plummet from falling perpendicularly, and a kindred experiment made by Mr. Cavendish in 1788. The experiments materialize too literally to be reasonable the physical attraction towards each other which is intellectually conceived to exist universally in physical bodies. If I am correctly informed, a fallacy has been discovered in the experiments that seemed to realize unverbally the intellectual conceptions of Newton, that diamonds and carbon are physically homogeneous. The only intellectual conceptions of which we ought to expect a physical realization, are such as are analogous to existing sensible perceptions: as, for instance, when we conceive of a newly discovered lake that it contains fish, our conception will be more likely to be realized physically than to be disappointed. In such conceptions, the intellect is performing its proper common-sense functions. So, also, when astronomers conceived that the great nebula in Orion was produced by indistinct stars, the intellect was only assimilating the nebula to what had previously been realized in the galaxy; hence, in that case also, the intellect was only performing its proper common-sense functions; and when the improved telescope of Lord Rosse subsequently materialized the conception, the materialization no way conflicts with the foregoing skepticism in relation to the pendulous experiments at Paris, etc.

LECTURE IX.

THE SAME SUBJECT CONTINUED.

CONTENTS.

1. The subjective nature of intellectual verbal conceptions, as contradistinguished from objective things, is urged upon our notice by the necromantic dilemmas to which the intellect organically arrives in predicating verbal conceptions to their ultimate results.
2. Conceptions of the intellect are organic, but not innate; their evolvement depending on accidental objective occurrences.

§ 1. Locke says, "that every person who possesses an idea of a foot, finds he can repeat the idea, and, joining it to the former, make the idea of two feet." "He may," says Locke, "continue the process without ever arriving at an end of his increase, whether the idea so enlarged be a foot, a mile, the diameter of the earth, or the orbis magnus." In my last Lecture I showed, that words which the intellect thus conceives on any occasion mean, physically, the sensibly perceptible objects only to which the words refer, and that the residue of meaning possessed by such intellectually conceived words is subjective, and exists in the organism of the intellect. I suppose this limitation in the sensible signification of words is not recognized in our speculations, and that we fallaciously deem the meaning of such words wholly physical. The error is very consequential, and surrounds our verbal knowledge with much mystery; just as the word ghost becomes mysterious when we deem it more than a verbal conception of the intellect, and especially when we mistake it for an objective existence. Our intellect, whose organization permits Locke's process of addition illimitably, and irrespectively of whether the addenda possess any physical archetype or not, may be likened to the wind, which is organized to blow whether any ships be wafted by it or not, and to fill the exposed sails of a ship whether the ship be moored to a dock or drifting on the ocean.

The intellectual organization, which permits the intellect to thus add whether the addenda be physical or not, is as useful as the physical organization which permits the wind to blow, whether any ship is, or not, propelled thereby; but the usefulness of neither organic process is impaired by our discrimination of what is subjective in the processes from what is objective. Indeed, Providence, as if to *force* on us the discrimination in the organism of the wind, compels our senses to note that a moored ship remains stationary, notwithstanding the continued bellying of her sails by the wind; and as if to force on us the discrimination in the organism of the intellect, between what is subjective and what is objective, compels the intellect to note that the continued process of addition leads ultimately to an extension without a terminus, or a terminus that no extension can reach; either result being as evincive that the process is not objective, but relates only to the organism of the intellect, as the immobility of the ship is evincive that the continued bellying of her sails relates only to the organism of the wind.

§ 2. Equally evincive with the above, of the distinction between sensibly objective things and intellectually subjective conceptions, is the intellectually conceived boundlessness of space. Soar in imagination ever so high, plunge ever so low, or extend laterally ever so far, the intellect can arrive at no end of its conception of space. Even if we imagine adamantine barriers in any direction, we are sure, says Locke, "that space exists to the extent of the barriers; and where the barriers terminate, space must commence again." But now, I say, if the foregoing results be not merely subjective (evincive of the organism of the intellect), a dilemma arises as necromantic as what we arrived at above, in extension; and we must admit the existence of an objective space without bounds, or objective bounds without space. To me the dilemma would be conclusive of the merely subjective character of the process, if I possessed no other criterion of its purely intellectual character. But a criterion exists entirely sufficient for me, irrespective of the above: whatever my senses cannot perceive must be intellectual, and cannot be physical. If I am incorrect in this, my whole treatise is a fallacy; for I assume throughout that words are unmeaning, except as they refer to some thing that is unverbal; and that unverbal things are heterogeneous, being intellectual, sensible, and emotional.

§ 3. That the earth needs no support is also an intellectual conception that depends for its unverbal signification on only the organism of the intellect; for if we adopt the Indian tradition, that the earth rests on an elephant, and the elephant on a tortoise, the intellect will still organically insist that the tortoise must rest on something, and so ad infinitum. Nor can the earth hang on any thing. The intellect may verbally suspend the earth with a chain from the sky, but the intellect will insist on a support to sustain the sky; and so again ad infinitum. The intellect is thus brought to the necromantic dilemma that usually attends such verbal processes; the intellect being compelled to choose between a conceived ultimate support that is unsupported, or a conceived ultimate suspension that is unsuspended. Modern astronomers select the latter alternative, and dismissing both Atlas and the elephant, conceive, intellectually, that the earth is suspended in space without a suspension on any thing, and mistake this logical subjective result of their intellectual organism for a physical reality: much like the fabled dog, who mistook for a rival quadruped what was only a subjective creation of the water into which he was looking.

§ 4. That every given time must have been preceded by a past, and must be followed by a future, are among the most inevitable conceptions of the intellect; but when the intellect proceeds illimitably with the past, the process brings us to the usual necromantic dilemma of a past without any antecedent, or an antecedent which had no beginning. Nor is our intellectual process with reference to a future any less necromantic, for we ultimately arrive at an end without any future, or a future without any end.

§ 5. That every thing required in its construction some material, is another conception that the intellect is organically incapable of avoiding; but when the intellect continues such conceptions abstractedly and illimitably, it arrives as usual at a necromantic dilemma, which presents us with a first material that was made out of nothing, or an eternity of things without any beginning to the series. The latter conclusion was held by the ancients; the creative power of Deity, said they, extends no farther than the arrangement of pre-existing materials. The moderns reject this circumscription of Divine power, and, taking the opposite alternative, insist that God created every thing out of nothing. Spinoza deemed both results unsatisfactory, and insisted that Deity was the material out of which all things are created. This he esteemed a great physical discovery of the intellect, and by which the maxim, nihil fit ex nihilo, was reconciled with the sole eternity of Deity. In view of such intellectual speculations which differ only in topics, not in kind, from any others that confound what pertains to the intellect subjectively with what pertains to the senses objectively, we may see that the wisdom of the world may well be accounted "foolishness with God." The intellect, by conceiving words in logical forms, cannot discover physical things which our senses have not revealed to us, any more than we can, "by taking thought, add a cubit to our stature."

§ 6. The intellect is organically compelled to conceive also, that nothing can exist without a maker; but when we intellectually predicate a maker illimitably, we arrive at a dilemma of the usual character, and must choose between a succession of makers without a beginning, or a beginning without a maker. The same may be repeated, severally, of the intellectual conceptions of a cause, a contriver, a designer; in each case we must choose between the conception of an endless succession of causes, contrivers, designers, without a first; or we must arrest the succession by an intellectually conceived first, that is uncaused, uncontrived, and undesigned, etc. A celebrated European philosopher, in lecturing on the above topics, was in the habit of prefacing his introduction by saying to his class, "Now, gentlemen, we will make God!" The remark was probably a sarcasm, for he belonged to the school which deems words insignificant when they refer to no sensible object; not seeing that intellectually conceived words derive an unverbal subjective meaning from the intellect whose aspirations and organism generally the conceived words manifest: just as the words scarlet, sweet, loud, fragrant, etc., derive an unverbal meaning from only the senses whose perceptions they designate; and just as the words anger, love, and pity, derive an unverbal meaning from only the internal feelings the words refer to.

§ 7. The indestructibility of matter is another conception of the intellect similar to the foregoing; the intellect being organically compelled to admit it, or to admit, ultimately, that something is nothing. The infinite divisibility of matter is another intellectual necessity of the same character; the intellect being organically necessitated to admit it, or to admit, ultimately, that a whole is not greater than a part. But while I endeavour to show that intellectually conceived words result from, and signify unverbally an intellectual organism, I mean not to assert that any verbal conceptions are innate, even when, like most or all the foregoing, they are found in all ages of the world and among all races of men. I claim only that given verbal conceptions are a result of the organism of the intellect when placed under given objective circumstances; and that the universality of any given verbal conception is a result of only the universality of the excitive objective circumstances; just as you will find language wherever you find human society—apple-eaters, wherever you find apples—climbers, wherever you find hills—swimmers and fishers, wherever you find water—and walkers every where, the earth being co-extensive with man.

LECTURE X.

OF THE UNFALLACIOUS PROSECUTION OF INQUISITION.

CONTENTS.

1. Retrospect of the preceding Lecture.
2. Questions analysed into an inquirer, inquiree, and object.
3. Each of the three is unverbally triform, and only verbally a unit.
4. The error exemplified of seeking sensibly what is only intellectual, and of seeking intellectually what is only sensible.
5. Inquisition is limited by the purview of our sensible, intellectual, and moral organisms.
6. All physical inquisition is unanswerable that is not within the purview of the senses; all intellectual inquisition is unanswerable that is not within the purview of the intellect; and all inquisition that relates to the internal feelings is unanswerable that is not within the purview of our consciousness therein.
7. Knowledge, except of language, is, in its ultimate form, unverbal, not verbal.
8. Conclusion.

Retrospect of the preceding Lecture.

§ 1. The preceding Lecture teaches that when the intellect premises that any thing is a contrivance, the intellect is organically constrained to see in the premises that they include the agency of a contriver; when the intellect premises that any thing is an effect, the intellect is organically constrained to conceive that the effect required a precedent cause; when the intellect premises that any thing is a whole, the intellect is organically compelled to conceive it is more than a part; when the intellect premises that A and B are severally equal to C, the intellect is constrained to conceive that A is equal to B; when the intellect premises that a mark which exists on a sandy shore is a footprint, the intellect is organically forced to conceive that some foot imprinted it; and when the intellect conceives that any thing is an existence, the intellect is organically compelled to conceive that the existence had a beginning, and must suffer a termination, etc. Wherein the cogency consists of given premises to compel the intellect to conceive therefrom given conclusions, I shall not inquire, for I am not writing a treatise on the intellect. The rationale of the process is, however, I think obvious; and in pages 164 to 206, of a former publication (entitled "A Treatise on Language," etc., published by the Harpers, of New York, for me in 1836), I manifested my views thereon elaborately; but the subject is not properly within my present design, which is limited to the unverbal meaning of words. Conclusions of the intellect, like the foregoing examples, are words, and only as such are they within my purview; and I have shown, in Lecture VIII., that, except what the senses can perceive, the ultimate unverbal meaning of intellectually conceived words is the organism of the intellect; just as the ultimate unverbal physical meaning of paralysis, beyond what is sensible, is the organism of our physical formation.

By means of our intellectual organism, my intellect is compelled to conceive, that what I behold in certain rocks and stones are the fossilized remains of an extinct species of animals that existed anterior to the Deluge; that certain existing ravines are extinct rivers; certain existing rocks, extinct volcanoes; certain distantly separated existing eminences, parts of a former entirety; that the centre of the earth is fire, and the surface of the earth a cool crust of what was originally a mass in fusion. Astronomy presents to my intellect premises which constrain it to conceive that the Asteroids are fragments of a large planet burst asunder by some unknown natural convulsion; though other premises will compel my intellect to conceive that the above is an unreasonable hypothesis, and to supersede it by conceiving that the Asteroids were made in their present form and for just the purposes they now subserve. A sermon will present to my intellect premises from which it will conceive the mode in which the dead are to be re-animated at the last day, and whether friends are to recognize each other, or remain unrecognized. The conclusions are all very reasonable, I may say. They accord with my intellectual organism as satisfactorily as a well prepared omelet accords with my physical organization. The conclusions signify, unverbally, the organism of my intellect, just as ventriloquism, whistling, talking, singing, and screaming, evince the organism of my vocal powers; and just as pain, smart, burn, etc., evince the organism of my physical formation. Now, I admit, that I can but postulate this doc trine. The doctrine is a verbal conception of my intellect as organic and subjective only, in its ultimate unverbal signification, as the other intellectual conceptions that I have alluded to, and possessing neither more unverbal significancy than they, nor less. I insist only, as positive knowledge, that intellectually conceived words can mean, physically, nothing but what is sensibly perceptible, and that all their other signification, except what is emotional, is intellectual, deriving its whole unverbal unction from the organism of the intellect.

But wherein is the above doctrine new? In this: other men fail to recognize that nearly every word may relate to three heterogeneous unverbal things. The fire, for instance, with which I am warming my boots, is sensible—the fire of lust, zeal, hate, opinion, etc., is an internal feeling; but the fire which the intellect conceives, verbally, in the centre of the earth, is an intellectual conception. The three fires are not homogeneous unverbally, though they are verbally, and I postulate no more. The difference between the three fires is precisely what it is; and thus to designate the difference is more accurate than any verbal designation—the unverbal difference being always ultimate to the verbal (underlying the verbal), select what verbal designation you may.

§ 2. I have now concluded all that I contemplated saying on the unverbal meaning of intellectually conceived words, and, indeed, of the unverbal meaning of words in every other use of them. I have endeavoured to only make men cease from contemplating unverbal things through the medium of language. I have endeavoured that unverbal things shall, on the contrary, occupy in creation the rank and precedence to which they are entitled as elder brothers of words. The unverbal thing to which the word man applies, is certainly older and more consequential than the word man: the unverbal thing should, therefore, be deemed the interpretation or exposition of the meaning of the word man; not, vice versâ, the word be deemed the interpretation of the unverbal thing. The like may be said of every other unverbal thing, and I have accordingly endeavoured that the unverbal multiplicity of any unverbal thing shall be no longer obscured by its verbal oneness; and that the unverbal diversities of any two things shall be no longer estimated by their verbal sameness or identity. These are, in brief, my whole doctrine, if you add thereto that I have throughout assumed for man a treble organization—sensible, intellectual, and emotional; and that every word of all languages must be bounded in its unverbal signification by the purview of our said three organisms, and be deemed as heterogeneous in its unverbal signification as the said three sets of organisms are heterogeneous in their functions. Words apply indiscriminately to the operations of the three species of organs; hence, words possess a verbal homogeneity that prevents us from seeing the heterogeneity of their unverbal meaning. Various phases of this verbal delusion I have adduced, but only for the purpose of illustrating the result on intellectual verbal speculations. With a final view to the same purpose, I will terminate the present speculations with an investigation of the unverbal signification of verbal inquisition. I have touched on no subject more practically useful, and on none so little understood; for as the eye sees every visible thing but itself, so questions have interrogated everything but interrogation.

§ 3. Every question presupposes an inquirer, an inquiree, and an object sought. The inquirer we will assume to be a man, and the inquiree a man also. Language deems every man a unit, but we have repeatedly shown that the nominal unit man is unverbally triune—sensible, intellectual, and internal feelings. Every question, therefore, addressed to *verbal* Peter, is addressed to three inconvertibly different *unverbal* Peters. We can readily conceive some mystification, were we questioning three Dromios, without suspecting their want of personal identity; but the mystification is greater with the three Peters that constitute the nominal unit of every inquiree; the three differing from each other even more heterogeneously and inconvertibly than the three Dromios—the senses being organically unable to perform the office of the intellect, and the intellect being organically unable to perform the offices of the senses, and the feelings being unable to perform the offices of the senses or the intellect. If we disregard this latent triplicity of the inquiree, our questions on any occasion may seek sensible information from the intellect, or intellectual information from the senses, etc.

§ 4. The difficulty becomes still more complicated, and the danger of mystification still more imminent, by the unverbal triplicity that characterizes the objects also of inquisition—the object sought being sometimes sensible information, sometimes intellectual information, and sometimes emotional information—three entirely distinct and inconvertibly different objects unverbally, but which language frequently deems an homogeneous unit.

Nearly all the perplexing questions of speculation are produced by verbal equivokes like the above. Our senses, for instance, cannot discover how the soul is united to the body, how effects are united to their causes, how our actions are united to our will, etc. But nothing in these disabilities ought to surprise us; the unions alluded to, being all conceptions of the intellect, are, by the nature of our organization, not discoverable by our senses, any more than the wings are which "riches take unto themselves when they fly away," or any more than sounds are discoverable by our sight, or colours by our ears. An astronomer, mystified by such indiscriminations, may admire, as a great physical enigma, that attraction, which pervades the universe, upholds the earth, and keeps the sun, moon, and planets in their respective orbits, can by no ingenuity of man be discovered in its physical personality, though its effects are ever present. The explanation of this enigma is precisely like the last. The attraction alluded to is a conception of the intellect, hence not discoverable by our senses any more than lead is digestible by our stomachs, thoughts tangible by our fingers, or dreams measurable by the gallon.

What we have said of attraction we may say of vitality. We are conscious of it, but its sensible personality constantly eludes our senses. The soul also, the mind, the intellect, severally elude all sensible searches—conscious of them continually, our senses can nowhere discover them. Such equivokes pass usually for profound mysteries; but all mystery vanishes when we know that the respective words name only conceptions of the intellect, and of course their meaning is not within the purview of our senses. The fallacy shows itself often in the science of medicine. Medical theories are intellectual conceptions; but physicians are continually striving to realize them physically; just as persons who seek to discover perpetual motion are endeavouring to realize sensibly a notion which exists only intellectually. The theories of diseases, of contagion, of generation, of alimentation, are severally conceptions of the intellect; and to the extent that the conception in each case is only intellectually conceived words, the mystery of our inability to realize it physically is a delusion. That inoculation will prevent small-pox, that vaccination is equivalent to inoculation, are conceptions of the intellect; but when sensible results conflict therewith in any particular, we need not be surprised—the theory and the sensible results belonging to two generically and inconvertibly different compartments of our knowledge; hence their conflict unverbally is no mysterious duality of any unverbal identity, the identity being only a verbal equivoke. A universal panacea, an elixir of life, a universal dissolvent, the transmutations of alchemy, are all conceptions of the intellect; but men who sought them as physical existences, were deluded by the verbal homogeneity of sensible objects and intellectual conceptions. That physical results habitually conform measurably to theoretical anticipations evinces only the beneficial design of our intellectual organization, and no way subverts the utility of our knowing the unverbal heterogeneity of intellectual conceptions and sensible perceptions.

§ 5. The intellect insists, imperatively and irresistibly, that every occurrence is the effect of some cause; hence, when a disease occurs, our intellect will insist that a cause has preceded it; but we are not always able to discover any sensible cause. We rarely recognize that the necessity which insists on a cause belongs only to the organism of our intellect, and that the undiscoverability of any sensible cause is not a *conflicting* fact, but an *additional* fact: both facts are equally true, but they relate to different organisms; the necessity for a cause being intellectual, while the undiscoverability of a cause is physical. This distinction I deem highly important, and it removes much speculative mystery; for when we deem a cause as much a physical necessity as it is an intellectual necessity, we are certainly involved in a delusive indiscrimination between the organic duality of our knowledge.

But I have been asked, whether the undiscoverability of

a physical cause is equivalent to the non-existence of a physical cause? I answer, that the two propositions possess different intellectual meanings, but not necessarily different physical meanings. Every proposition means physically the physical facts only to which it refers; hence, to affirm of any given occurrence, that no physical cause exists therefor or to affirm that no physical cause therefor is discoverable, will in both cases possess but one physical meaning, if they both refer to the same physical fact. I am anxious to manifest only that when we deem a cause as much a physical necessity as it is an intellectual necessity, we are identifying things that are generically different, and hence we are mystifying our knowledge by means of a misunderstanding of the nature of language. We are viewing unverbal things through the veil which, the oracle says, has never been taken off.

The intellect will insist also, that the generation of a fœtus, the germination of a seed, the assimilation of nourishment into the substances of our body, etc., must result from some processes analogous to sensible creative operations; and when such processes are not discoverable sensibly, we deem the processes peculiarly mysterious; but our knowledge will be less sophistical by understanding the generic intransmutability of intellectual conceptions into sensible things, and hence, that the disagreement of the two, as above, is only a manifestation of our knowledge in its unverbal truth.

That on the earth some point exists where magnetic attraction is fixedly located, is a conception of the intellect; and such a locality is said to have been discovered physically by some late Arctic navigator, though I much doubt it. The discovery will, however, only show the possibility of a sensible realization of an intellectual conception; just as the search after hidden treasure, founded on a dream, may also be occasionally realized. The cases are, however, wholly different, inasmuch as the intellect was organized to prompt and aid our physical researches, and hence, intellectual conceptions of a given analogy to sensible perceptions are often realized sensibly; while dreams were not made to facilitate the discovery of buried treasures, and are rarely realized.

The intellect conceives that all sensible perceptions are but qualities of some physical substratum. What this intellectually conceived substratum is physically, philoso phers say the senses cannot discover—the senses being able to know only the effects produced in them by this undiscoverable substratum. That such a substance exists, and that no efforts of the senses can discover it, seems very mysterious till we find that it is only a conception of the intellect; hence, like thought, it is organically out of the purview of the senses, and to say we cannot discover it, is only equivalent to saying that the senses cannot discover what is not sensible. Language speaks, however, of substance, as it would speak of a horse; and when we look only verbally, the inability of the senses to discover the intellectually conceived substance seems as mysterious as would be our inability to discover a postulated horse.

The intellect conceives that terrestrial creation constitutes a chain, which ascends by links of so insensible a gradation from unorganized matter to man, the climax of organized materiality, that we cannot discover, sensibly, where inorganic matter ends and organic commences, where vegetable life ends, and animal commences, or where any species of animality terminates and another species commences—including even the link which separates man from some other animals. Our inability to discover the postulated links and gradations constitutes the mystery. But we have discovered them, or we should be unable to talk about them! This explains the mystery: what we have discovered are intellectual, but what we cannot discover are sensible. We cannot discover, sensibly, the chain, links, gradations, etc., that we conceive intellectually. The inability proceeds from no defect of the senses, from no inscrutableness of unverbal things, but simply from the heterogeneity of our organisms. What is conceived intellectually, and what is perceived sensibly, may be nominally identical and verbally homogeneous; but, unverbally, they belong to different worlds—the world of the intellect, and the world of the senses. Instead of contrasting the discoverability and undiscoverability as mysterious antagonists, we should note the antagonism as parts of our experimental knowledge, and thereby obey the ancient injunction, "Know thyself." And here we may note how insidiously, in cases like the above, we play a game of bo-peep with the word "discover," using it at one moment to designate an intellectual operation, and the next moment to designate a sensible operation, without recognizing that we are talking of two processes that are unverbally heterogeneous, though verbally homogeneous.

In a treatise, entitled "The Theory of Agreeable Sensations," a recent writer says: "Actors, when they either laugh or weep, affect spectators with the sensations which the drama expresses; but who can discover the mechanism by which the fibres of the actor's brain transmit themselves to that of the spectators!" The discovery spoken of as mysteriously impracticable is, of course, to be physical; while the things to be discovered are only conceptions of the intellect, namely, "the mechanism by which the fibres of the actor's brain transmit themselves to the brain of other persons." The delusion becomes apparent the moment we penetrate through the homogeneity of words, and analyze unverbal things into their generic differences. In the same fallacious way we may marvel that we cannot find, sensibly, how animal life commences—how something becomes nothing, or nothing becomes something—how external objects or their impressions are carried by the nerves to the brain, etc.; and for the simple reason, that the things to be found sensibly, are not sensible but intellectual conceptions.

§ 6. The great instruments of verbal inquisition are the words *what* and *how;* as when we say, *what* is gravity?—*how* is the soul united to the body? The moment we clearly understand the "what" and "how" as inquiring after some physical thing, we see why we cannot tell what gravity is personally—its personality being not a physical thing, but a conception of the intellect; hence, the question is equivalent to asking what physical thing is a thing that is not physical. We may repeat the same remarks of how the soul is united to the body. The question, as usually propounded, is equivalent to asking what physical modus operandi is a modus operandi that is not physical.

§ 7. I discover in the work of Auguste Comte, as translated by Harriet Martineau (the only form in which I have seen any work of his), that he deprecates all inquiries like the above, they being, as he thinks, beyond the purview of human knowledge. He says: "As to what weight and attraction are, we have nothing to do with that question, for it is not a matter of knowledge at all." That so recent a philosopher as Comte, so acute, learned, and discriminating, is still so bewildered by the homogeneity of words, as to mistake an error of inquisition for a mystery transcending human knowledge, is to me an encouraging proof that the present work is not unnecessary. He says, again: "Mr. Fourier, in his fine researches on heat, has given us the most important and precise laws of the phenomena of heat, and many large and new truths, without once inquiring into the nature of heat, as his predecessors had done, when they disputed about calorific matter and the action of an universal ether." Certainly, if we are to mistake for physical the "calorific matter" and the "universal ether," which are only intellectual conceptions, Mr. Fourier was wise in not disputing about such delusive misconstructions; but his researches would not have been injured, they would have been more definite, had he stated that his inquiries were not directed to the physical personality of heat, as contradistinguished from heat's sensible manifestations—such physical personality being not physical, but only a conception of the intellect.

Like the above is the assertion of Comte, that we are "without data about the constitution of bodies." I infer from the context, that he means we possess no physical data in relation to the constituents which the intellect conceives to be the components of physical bodies. Of course we possess no such physical data, and never can possess any; the components being not physical, but intellectual conceptions. He also quotes, approvingly, somebody as saying, that the "miniature picture" which is painted on the retina of the eye in vision, and by which distant external objects are brought to the notice of the intellect, cannot avail the intellect, unless the intellect possesses another eye to see the miniature. This sarcasm is pretty, but far prettier is an elucidation of the mistake which deems the optical theory in relation to the miniature a physical modus operandi, instead of only an intellectual conception. Our indiscrimination between intellectual conceptions and sensible perceptions, seems proportioned in degree to the marvel that can be produced by the indiscrimination. Every person talks of the above optical theory with apparently an entire unsuspicion of the difference between what is sensibly perceptible in relation thereto, and what is intellectually conceived. The same may be said of the theoretical agency of our nerves in general, in fetching information from external objects to our brain, and carrying volitions from the brain to the other members of our body; of our supporting severally on our bodies a physical pressure of fourteen tons of atmosphere; of being physically whirled through space every hour about a thousand miles in one direction, and about fifty-eight thousand miles in another direction. Infidelity sneers at the prophet Joshua, and we laugh at all the ancients who supposed the earth was at rest, and that the sun and other celestial bodies revolved around our earth, as we now conceive that the earth revolves around the sun; and no man can be found who supposes that the difference is not physical, and that we differ from the ancients in only our intellectual conceptions on the subject. Our internal feelings relish the indiscrimination which we practise between what is intellectual and what is physical; and to this encouragement, more than to any obtuseness of the intellect, we doubtless owe the undisturbed prevalence of the indiscrimination; just as we owe to the same encouragement feats of legerdemain, the tales of the Arabian Nights, and the growing tendency to fabulize all history and all biography. We relish the equivoke in the Arabian tales and in legerdemain, though our intellect detects it; and we may continue to relish also our historical, biographical, and our scientific indiscriminations between what is physical and what is intellectual, after our intellect shall detect them; and continue their employment as a provocative to reading and to scientific studies, an end for which, more than any other probably, they have so long remained unchallenged.

How mysterious are the ways of Providence! This is a familiar expression. Physical events will not conform to our conceptions of the order in which they ought to transpire, and we deem the physical variance quite mysterious, and ask the intellect what the variance means. It means that we fail to discriminate the generic difference between intellectual conceptions and sensible perceptions. The intellect will conceive according to either its organic or indoctrinated tendencies—its conceptions being subjective, not objective; hence the variance between our conception of how events ought to transpire, and our sensible perception of the order in which they occur, are no way antagonistic to each other—the two belonging to different branches of our ego. Would we understand accurately the "ways of Providence," we must learn them from our sensible experience if we desire a sensible fruition of the search; but if we desire an intellectual fruition, we must accept such intellectually conceived words as different intellects will conceive under different conditions or under different indoctrinations. The above is what my intellect conceives on the subject, and I give it for nothing more.

§ 8. Having thus given many examples of questions which seek sensibly what is intellectual, I will adduce some of the correlative errors of seeking intellectually for something that is physical. How mysterious, we exclaim, is death! What can it be? We desire the intellect to tell us what death is physically—the death which the intellect conceives. This desire in us to have the intellect materialize its conceptions of death, and, indeed, all its conceptions, is organic in our *feelings*, and is the source of all theories and hypotheses. That this organic tendency is useful we know, from the practical purposes which theories subserve, and from the faith we possess that all our organic powers and aspirations subserve important practical utilities. But while we thus accord importance to such inquiries of the intellect as ask of it what death is in material personality?—what life, spirit, mind, soul are respectively? —we shall gain nothing by not recognizing that, though the intellect may conceive some theory or hypothesis by which to assimilate its conceptions of death, etc., to personalities sensibly perceptible, yet the theoretical assimilation will still be intellectual, not physical. The inherent distinction, and the inconvertible difference, are insurmountable between the unverbal things of the three great departments into which are divisible all we know or can know. Language can assimilate the three heterogeneous things verbally, but not unverbally; language can transmute unverbal things one into another verbally; but, unverbally, they are untransmutable.

"When," says Comte, "any attempt has been made to explain what is attraction and weight, it has ended only in saying, that attraction is universal weight, and that weight is terrestrial attraction: that is, that the two orders of phenomena are identical, which is the point from which the question set out." Of course, if you ask the intellect what (physical thing understood) weight and attraction are, the intellect can answer by only some intellectually conceived words. If you desire any other answer—especially if you desire a physical answer—your question must be directed, not to the intellect, but to the senses. If we want figs, we must not go to a thistle; and if we want thistles, we must not seek them on fig-trees: this obvious scriptural precept applies to our unverbal knowledge in its threefold heterogeneity.

"The little bodies which compose water, and which are so loose one from another that the least force separates them, and which bodies, from their perpetual motion, seem to possess no cohesion, will unite under a sharp cold, and not be separated without great force." I quote the above from Locke, who adds, "that he who could make known the cement that makes the little bodies adhere so closely together, would discover a great and yet unknown secret."

What cement makes the particles of frozen water adhere together so closely, is the above question mooted by Locke. His intellect conceived that water was composed of "little particles," and that ice was produced by some "cement" which solidified the conceived particles. The intellectually conceived particles and cement he, being misled by language, deemed homogeneous with physical particles and physical cement. This was error number one, and under the influence thereof, he deemed very mysterious that his senses could neither feel nor see in ice the little particles nor the cement that his intellect conceived to be therein.

Baffled in his ability to thus discover sensibly what are only intellectual, he committed error number two, by seeking from his intellect the physical personality of the fallaciously assumed physical particles and cement. But his intellect could, of course, yield him no perceptions thereof; his intellect could yield him only its own intellectual conceptions thereon; and thus he deemed the particles and cement " a great and yet unknown mystery." Had Locke said that in his mind was some thought that no man's senses could discover, no person would have suffered surprise, the terms of the proposition evincing sufficiently that he alluded to an intellection; but when Locke speaks of cement, particles, etc., the threefold meanings which such words can bear, unverbally, prevents us from seeing that Locke is employing them in only their intellectual meaning, and hence necessarily, that our senses cannot discover them.

§ 9. Hume says, " Our senses inform us of the colour, weight, and consistence of bread; but neither sense nor reason can inform us of the *qualities* which fit bread for the nourishment and support of the human body." Certain qualities are here postulated which neither the senses nor the intellect can inform us of. How, then, do we know they exist? We must know from the intellect; for if the senses cannot discover them, they are intellectually conceived qualities, and this accounts for why we cannot be informed of them by the senses. But why not by the reason or intellect? Because we require the answer to be physical, consequently we cannot obtain it through the intellect. The intellect and the senses can inform us what fits bread for the nourishment and support of the body; but we must ask from the senses only sensible information, and from the intellect only intellectual information; and not permit the duplicity of the word "qualities" to mislead us into an inquiry after sensible qualities from the intellect, or intellectually conceived qualities from the senses.

Locke says, further: "Our body possesses the power of communicating motion by impulse, and our soul the power of exciting motion by thought; but if we would inquire how the soul and body produce these effects, we are entirely in the dark." Let us separate the above soul and body. The body communicates motion by impulse, but "of the modus operandi we are entirely in the dark." The question, therefore, must inquire after some modus operandi that is not sensible, but an intellectually conceived modus operandi; and we cannot find it sensibly of course. But we cannot find "how our soul excites motion by thought." The modus operandi that is now sought is physical, and of course we cannot find it intellectually. In ordinary inquiries, however, of the intellect after a physical modus operandi, the intellect will conceive a theory which will verbally satisfy our inquiry; but when the inquiry relates to how "the soul excites by thought the physical motion of our limbs," the process of volition, which is the object of the inquiry, is so unique that sensible experience supplies the intellect with no sensible materials out of which it can conceive a satisfactory theoretical modus operandi. Our bodily power to communicate sensible motion by impulse is equally unique; hence, in both cases, an intellectually conceived modus operandi is equally difficult, and the difficulty is the fallacious mystery.

We cannot find how "light passes through solid crystal;" that is, the senses cannot perceive the modus operandi which the intellect conceives, and which, of course, is not sensible, but an intellectual conception; or we may reverse the enigma, and seek in the intellect for a physical modus operandi; and of course we cannot find it, unless we accept therefor a theory, and mistake it for a physical revelation.

§ 10. I have, as yet, said nothing of questions in which the object sought relates to an internal feeling. Burke inquires, "Why visible objects of great dimensions are sublime?" Let us assume that he meant an internal feeling by the word sublime. The reason, then, why visible objects of great dimensions excite such a feeling, is like inquiring why sugar excites the taste that we call sweetness. We are so organized as to have the feeling of sublimity excited by what does excite it, and the taste of sweetness excited by what does excite it. But Burke meant more. He wanted the intellect to find some modus operandi, and his intellect accordingly conceived a mode which I will not quote; but it answered his question in the way he desired an answer, and he was accordingly satisfied. But another person may not be satisfied, but may want to find sensibly Burke's intellectually conceived modus operandi; and being unable to discover it sensibly, may deem the inability a great mystery.

§ 11. What is pride, vanity, ambition, wisdom, wit, folly, anger, rage? Books have been written to answer these questions, not, however, by enabling our consciousness to recognize the internal feeling which each word names, but to state what the intellect conceives of the materiality and corporeity of the various personalities—for such the intellect conceives them to be; and the writers seem to possess no suspicion that the intellect can tell no more in the premises than its conceptions thereon. They evidently impute to the feeling named anger, and the intellectual conception of its personality, etc., an homogeneity and oneness that exists verbally only. The like may be said of each other nominal feeling.

§ 12. Can we prove the existence of an external universe? Can a man prove his own existence? Nothing which philosophy has debated is perhaps so mysterious as these questions; but the whole mystery exists in the duplicity, or rather triplicity, of the word *prove.* When it refers to the intellect, it alludes to an intellectual proof; when it refers to the senses, it means a sensible proof; and when it refers to the internal feelings, it means an emotional proof, a feeling of consciousness. When, therefore, Descartes commenced his investigations with a determination to assent to nothing that he could not prove, and began with the logical enthymeme, "I think, therefore I am," he was alluding to an intellectual proof. "But," replies Dr. Reid, "how do you prove that you think? If you assume this without proof, you may assume your own existence without proof." Dr. Reid maintains that only consciousness can prove the existence of an external universe, or of a man's own personal existence. Of course, therefore, Dr. Reid is alluding to an emotional proof—not to the proof that Descartes alluded to. "But," says a subsequent writer, "how do you prove the existence of consciousness of which you speak?" He doubtless referred to a sensible proof, and consciousness is not sensibly perceptible, nor is the cogency of logic sensibly perceptible; therefore, this writer can maintain that neither the external world, nor his own personality, is provable by consciousness or logic.

Of the unverbal limitation of verbal inquisition.

§ 1. Having, I hope, sufficiently shown the errors which are involved in verbal inquisition, when we disregard the heterogeneity which exists among unverbal things that are verbally homogeneous, I will subjoin a few remarks on the limits of verbal inquisition. To inquire of the blind in relation to colours, or of the deaf in relation to sounds, is known to be ineffectual; but we know not with equal clearness that all inquisition is bounded by man's intellect, his senses, and his internal feelings; and that any question that relates not to one of these three departments of our ego is as unanswerable as an inquiry of the blind and deaf above alluded to, and for precisely the same reason. I will, however, assume as a result, now sufficiently evident, that every question is unanswerable whose object is not within the purview of some one of our three organic inquirees; as, for instance, the question asked ironically by Sterne: "What if the sun should wander from the zodiac?" But some intellects may be able to conceive consequences from even such premises; hence, to them, the question of Sterne will not be unanswerable *intellectually*, though it is unanswerable *sensibly* and *morally*. Indeed, language can frame no question that the intellect may not answer with some conceived words, even were we to ask the effect which would result should a spark of fire fall amid the satellites of Jupiter. This illimitability of intellectual inquisition we can more readily understand when we consider that the intellect which asks questions is the intellect that answers; the questioner and questionee being, therefore, identical in personality, are identical in purview.

Examples are, however, easily given of unanswerable physical inquisition; as, for instance, what is the shape of a taste, or the colour of a sound? These questions are unanswerable, by reason that their object, if you admit it to be physical information, is not within the purview of the senses—the senses being the inquiree to whom the questions are addressed. In addition, therefore, to the general postulate, that all solvable inquisition is limited to the purview of our senses, our intellect, and our internal feelings, we arrive at the more definite conclusion, that all physical inquisition is unanswerable, that is not within the purview of our senses; all inquisition that relates to the internal feelings is unanswerable, that is not within the purview of the internal feelings; and all intellectual inquisition is unanswerable, that is not within the purview of the intellect—if any such intellectual inquisition can be conceived.

§ 2. A distinction, not noted above, may be made between an insignificant question and a question that is unanswerable. To ask what is the shape of a taste is unanswerable, if the information sought be physical—such information not being within the purview of our senses: still the question may be significant to the intellect. All verbal inquisition is thus embarrassed with the threefold reference of words to our threefold organization; unless we avoid the embarrassment by postulating which of our three organisms is to be the inquiree, and to which of our three organisms belongs the object that is sought by the inquiry. A man, while recently perforating the earth in search of a salt spring, came to water from which ascended a stream of inflammable gas; and he employs a newspaper to solicit from philosophers an answer as to whether the gas proceeds from a decomposition of the water, or exists independently thereof. The querist, probably, never reflected whether he was seeking an answer from the intellects of philosophers or from their senses, though the answers of the two inquirees must differ generically, the intellect being as unable to originate sensible information as the senses are to originate intellectual conceptions.

In certain essays on human knowledge (Ogilvie's Essays), published in New York some years since, the author asserts that "he will endeavour to explain the extent to which mind and matter are knowable." The phrase "mind and matter" is not deemed by him to be limited in its signification by our knowledge; but our knowledge is deemed capable of teaching us a certain portion only of the signification of the phrase. What a curious mystification! We know "mind and matter" beyond the extent to which we can know them. The mystification, however, terminates the moment we analyze the word "*know*," and find it possesses three wholly different and inconvertible meanings—sensible, intellectual, and emotional. We can know mind and matter intellectually, beyond what we can know them sensibly; and this, instead of being mysterious, is a simple exposition of our triform organization. The verbal announcement of the result seems mysterious by reason that we fail to postulate that the organs which know mind and matter are not the organs which know them not. The different organs are like two Dromios; one may tell us he knows certain facts of mind and matter, while the other may tell us he knows them not. The contradiction seems mysterious, if we suppose the two answerers to be identical; but the contradiction is simple enough when we know their distinct individuality.

The significance of language can be made as capacious as the purview of our organisms, but not more capacious. I may deem very mysterious that I cannot taste the flavour of moonshine, nor smell its odour; nor feel the texture of the molecules of which it is composed. If I catch a handful of them, they elude my grasp before I can convey them into a dark closet for closer inspection. This is exceedingly wonderful to a person who sees not that the flavour which I cannot taste, the odour which I cannot smell, the molecules' texture and particles which I cannot catch and feel, are all intellectual conceptions, not sensible things; and hence, of course, I can neither taste, smell, catch, nor feel them. The true mystery is, not that I cannot accomplish such requirements, but that the error of such a use of language has remained so long unexplained.

I have discussed the present topic too briefly; but I hope sufficiently to manifest that no man can inquire intelligibly without he knows whether he is seeking sensible information, or some intellectual conception, or some emotional feeling; and that no man can answer understandingly without he knows which of his three organic inquirees is to furnish the answer; and I may add, that no answer can be correctly interpreted till we know to which class of unverbal things the answer refers—to the things of the intellect, the senses, or the emotional feelings. I referred in my preface to the ancient oracle that was engraved on the pavement of a temple of Minerva, "I am all that has been, that is, and that shall be, and none among mortals has hitherto taken off my veil." I may not have succeeded in the attempt which the oracle announces as never having been accomplished, but I fully believe the accomplishment will be consummated when the mode of interpreting language is correctly understood.

The ultimate unverbal signification of words.

§ 1. I am now arrived at the last topic of my analysis of words—their ultimate unverbal signification. I have anticipated the topic in several places, but it properly belongs here, and unless we possess definite knowledge on the subject, we shall not know when verbal inquisition is properly at an end. Would we know, for instance, the unverbal meaning of the word anger, the feeling itself alone can yield us the information. It can say as God said from the flaming bush, "I am that I am," no verbal answer being free from fallacy. We may repeat the like of every other internal feeling, and when consciousness presents the feeling unverbally, the question is answered unverbally, which is the only answer that cannot deceive—the only answer that is not fallacious.

§ 2. So the ultimate unverbal signification of every word that names anything sensible, is the sensible perception itself to which the word refers. Our ultimate unverbal sensible knowledge of death, for instance, our senses alone can reveal to us in their mute unverbal revelations. And what we have thus said of death applies equally to every other sensible thing, and to all sensible agencies and modes of operation. Would we know the agency of our brain over our actions, the agency of electricity over matter, the agency of volition over our limbs, we may employ our senses in every way we can on these several subjects, and every perception they yield is an answer to our investigations—an answer unverbal and not ambiguous, and the only answer that is unfallacious.

§ 3. If, however, we want an intellectual answer as to what death is, or what anger is, or how volition acts on our limbs, etc., we must accept such intellectually conceived words as the intellect shall be able to present to us in the premises; and they will constitute the answer of the intellect—but not the ultimate answer—for behind all such intellectually conceived words exists the organism of the intellect; in which organism alone exists the unverbal meaning of intellectually conceived words. In the discovery of such an ultimate unverbal signification of intellectually conceived words, lies, probably, the original distinction between nominalists and realists—realists recognizing such an unverbal signification, and nominalists not delving quite deep enough to reach it.

§ 4. Finally, our unverbal knowledge consists of what our senses can perceive, what our internal feelings can manifest, and what our intellect (interpreted as above) can conceive; and if we keep each class distinct, so as not to confound them by means of their verbal transmutability into each other, we shall possess our knowledge devoid of all fallacy; and shall no longer deem perplexingly mysterious, that we cannot discover sensibly what we conceive intellectually, or commit any kindred solecism; and we shall pass through life exempt from all mystery except the one great common mystery that attaches equally and alike to all we know, or can know—an ennobling consummation abundantly remunerative of all the intellectual labour it may cost the man who shall attain it. The world also, when the consummation shall become general (and general it must become at some future day), will understand distinctly the kind of information it is seeking on any occasion, and by which of our three organisms to seek it; and will look back at our present indiscrimination of unverbal heterogeneities in things verbally homogeneous, etc., etc., as a man looks back at the speculations of his childhood. Then will be known the new logic and critic which Locke began to suspect at the close of his Essay on the Human Understanding, when he said (in Book IV., chap. 21, § 4), "Perhaps if ideas and words were distinctly weighed, and duly considered, they would afford us another sort of logic and critic than what we have hitherto been acquainted with." What a painful, but too late a dawning of light, must this have been! He had just completed his great intellectual labour "concerning the Human Understanding," when he probably began to see that what is unverbal in human knowlege reveals itself to us spontaneously, and in the most unmistakable form; and that all about which men can differ, and about which he had been differing from others, must relate to only the words with which we shall talk and speculate concerning unverbal things, and the mode in which words shall be interpreted into the unverbal things to which the words refer.

STANDARD EDUCATIONAL WORKS,

PUBLISHED BY

D. APPLETON & CO.,

443 & 445 BROADWAY, N. Y

☞ We present below a list of our Educational Works, classified according to the grade of school for which they are adapted. In some cases, in which the book is equally suited to different grades, the title is repeated. For convenience of reference, the works in foreign languages, ancient and modern, are arranged by themselves, without reference to this classification. A detailed description of each book may be found in our new Descriptive Catalogue, sent free on application to the publishers

ENGLISH.

Primary School Text-Books.

WEBSTER'S ELEMENTARY SPELLING-BOOK. "The National Standard," of which more than one million copies are sold annually,...................$ 10

WRIGHT'S PRIMARY LESSONS. A neat illustrated little volume of 144 pages; being a Primary Spelling-Book and Reader happily combined,...... 12½

FIRST THOUGHTS: Or, Beginning to Think. A neat little volume with numerous illustrations, teaching common things in a pleasing manner. 12mo., 109 pages,.. 50

MANDEVILLE'S NEW "PRIMARY" READER. Beautifully illustrated. 12mo.,.. 18¾

MANDEVILLE'S NEW "SECOND" READER,............................ 14

CORNELL'S FIRST STEPS IN GEOGRAPHY. Designed for young children in schools and families,.................................... 2[illegible]

CORNELL'S PRIMARY GEOGRAPHY. Small 4to., 96 pages, with maps and illustrations,.. 5[illegible]

THE CHILD'S FIRST HISTORY OF AMERICA. By the author of "Little Dora." Square 18mo., illustrated.................................... [illegible]

PERKINS' PRIMARY ARITHMETIC: Containing Intellectual and Written Arithmetic.. 21

RICORD'S YOUTH'S GRAMMAR: Or, Easy Lessons in Etymology. A neat 12mo. 25

QUACKENBOS' FIRST LESSONS IN COMPOSITION: Combining Composition and Grammar.. 5[illegible]

COE'S PRIMARY DRAWING CARDS. In Ten Parts with Instructions, each 2[illegible]

COE AND SCHELL'S ELEMENTARY DRAWING CARDS. In Three Parts, with Instructions, each.. 1

Intermediate School Text-Books.

MANDEVILLE'S NEW SERIES OF READING BOOKS. Illustrated..	$ 12½
" SECOND READER	19
" THIRD READER	38
" FOURTH READER	56
" FIFTH READER	75
ROBBINS' CLASS-BOOK OF POETRY. By the author of "Popular Lessons"	75
ROBBINS' GUIDE TO KNOWLEDGE. A Reading-book adapted to young persons	63
REID'S ENGLISH DICTIONARY: With Derivations, &c.	1 00
OWEN'S WRITING-BOOKS. Complete in Three Parts, each	12½
QUACKENBOS' FIRST LESSONS IN COMPOSITION: Combined with Grammar	50
CORNELL'S PRIMARY GEOGRAPHY	50
CORNELL'S INTERMEDIATE do.	67
CORNELL'S GRAMMAR-SCHOOL GEOGRAPHY	90
COVELL'S DIGEST OF ENGLISH GRAMMAR: Synthetical and Analytical	50
CHAMPLIN'S CONCISE PRACTICAL ENGLISH GRAMMAR: With Exercises in Analysis and Parsing. 12mo. 219 pages	84
HAND-BOOK OF ANGLO-SAXON ROOT-WORDS	50
" OF ANGLO-SAXON DERIVATIVES	75
" OF THE ENGRAFTED WORDS OF THE ENGLISH LANGUAGE	1 00
MARSHALL'S BOOK OF ORATORY. Part I	62
" " Part II	1 00
PERKINS' ELEMENTARY ARITHMETIC	42
" PRACTICAL do.	62
" HIGHER do.	75
" ELEMENTS OF ALGEBRA	75
" ELEMENTS OF GEOMETRY	1 00
CROSBY'S FIRST LESSONS IN GEOMETRY. On the plan of "Colburn's Intellectual Arithmetic." Small 12mo	38
QUACKENBOS' SCHOOL HISTORY OF THE UNITED STATES. Illustrated	1 00
KIRKLAND (MRS.) PERSONAL MEMOIRS OF GEO. WASHINGTON. 12mo. School edition	1 00
SEWELL'S FIRST HISTORY OF ROME	50
" FIRST HISTORY OF GREECE	63
MARKHAM'S SCHOOL HISTORY OF ENGLAND	75
MANGNALL'S HISTORICAL QUESTIONS	1 00
GREEN'S PRIMARY BOTANY	75
COMINGS' CLASS-BOOK OF PHYSIOLOGY	1 00
" COMPANION to Same. By same author. Containing the plates of Class-Book, with questions. 12mo	50
YOUMANS' CLASS-BOOK OF CHEMISTRY. 1 Vol., 12mo	75
" CHEMICAL CHART ON ROLLERS. 5 feet by	5 00
" CHEMICAL ATLAS. 4to	2 00
QUACKENBOS' NATURAL PHILOSOPHY. Illustrated	1 00
KEIGHTLEY'S MYTHOLOGY. 18mo. An Abridgment of the author's large work	49

JAEGER'S ZOOLOGY. Very elementary. Designed for common schools....$ 42

PALMER'S BOOK-KEEPING. Elementary, with Practical Examples. 12mo., 86 pages. Blank to Same, each........ 19

OTIS' EASY LESSONS IN LANDSCAPE DRAWING. In Six Parts.
Parts I, II, III, each........ 25
Parts IV, V, and VI, each........ 37
The Six Parts bound in one........ $ 25

OTIS' DRAWING-BOOKS OF ANIMALS. In Five Parts. I and II, each.. 25
Part III........ 36
Parts IV and V, each........ 50
The Five Parts in one........ $ 25

High-School & Academic Text-Books.

MANDEVILLE'S READING AND ORATORY. Large 12mo........ $1 00

MARSHALL'S BOOK OF ORATORY. 12mo. 500 pages........ 1 00

SHAKESPERIAN READER. By Prof. Hows. 12mo. 447 pages........ 1 25

ROEMER'S POLYGLOT READERS. Five Volumes. Vol. I., composed of English extracts; Vol. II., their translation into French; Vol. III., German; Vol. IV., Spanish; and Vol. V., Italian........each 1 25

HOMER'S ILIAD. Translated by Cowper, revised by Southey, with Notes by Dwight. One large vol., 12mo. Cloth........ 1 25

PYCROFT'S COURSE OF ENGLISH READING. 12mo. Cloth........ 75

CORNELL'S GRAMMAR-SCHOOL GEOGRAPHY........

CORNELL'S HIGH-SCHOOL GEOGRAPHY AND COMPANION ATLAS.. 1 75

PERKINS' HIGHER ARITHMETIC. 324 pages........ 75
" ELEMENTS OF ALGEBRA........ 75
" TREATISE ON ALGEBRA........ 1 50
" ELEMENTS OF GEOMETRY........ 1 00
" PLANE AND SOLID GEOMETRY........ 1 50
" PLANE TRIGONOMETRY........ 1 50

GILLESPIE'S LAND SURVEYING: Theoretical and Practical........ 2 00

COVELL'S DIGEST OF ENGLISH GRAMMAR........ 50

QUACKENBOS' ADVANCED COMPOSITION AND RHETORIC........ 1 00

SPALDING'S HISTORY OF ENGLISH LITERATURE........ 1 00

GRAHAM'S ENGLISH SYNONYMS........ 1 00

REID'S ENGLISH DICTIONARY. With Derivations, &c........ 1 00

OTIS' DRAWING-BOOKS OF ANIMALS........ 2 25
" " " LANDSCAPE........ 2 25

YOUMANS' CLASS-BOOK OF CHEMISTRY........ 75
" ATLAS OF CHEMISTRY........ 2 00
" CHART OF CHEMISTRY; on rollers........ 5 00
" HAND-BOOK OF HOUSEHOLD SCIENCE. A Popular Account of Heat, Light, Aliment, and Cleansing, in their Scientific Principles and Domestic Applications........ 1 00

JOHNSTON'S CHEMISTRY OF COMMON LIFE. Numerous Illustrations. 2 vols., 12mo........ 2 00

GREEN'S CLASS-BOOK OF BOTANY........ 75

COMINGS' CLASS-BOOK OF PHYSIOLOGY........ 1 00

DWIGHT'S INTRODUCTION TO THE STUDY OF ART........ 1 00

QUACKENBOS' ILLUSTRATED SCHOOL-HISTORY OF THE UNITED STATES........ 1 00

TAYLOR'S MANUAL OF ANCIENT AND MODERN HISTORY........ 2 25

PUTZ AND ARNOLD'S MEDIÆVAL GEOGRAPHY AND HISTORY.... $1
" MODERN GEOGRAPHY AND HISTORY........ 1
GUIZOT'S HISTORY OF CIVILIZATION..................................
KOEPPEN'S HISTORICAL GEOGRAPHY. "The World in the Middle Ages." 2 vols., 12mo.. 2 00
BOJESEN AND ARNOLD'S MANUAL OF GRECIAN AND ROMAN ANTIQUITIES.. 1 00
ARNOLD'S HISTORY OF ROME.. 3 00
" LECTURES ON MODERN HISTORY........................... 1 25
KOHLRAUSCH'S HISTORY OF GERMANY.............................. 1 50
A NEW ORIGINAL WORK ON CHRONOLOGY—for every day in the year. 1 volume.. 2 00
COUSIN'S LECTURES ON THE HISTORY OF PHILOSOPHY............ 3 00
" " ON THE TRUE, THE BEAUTIFUL, AND THE GOOD.. 1 50
LEWES' BIOGRAPHICAL HISTORY OF PHILOSOPHY. 2 vols., 8vo. 1857 3 00
WHEWELL'S HISTORY OF THE INDUCTIVE PHILOSOPHY. 2 vols., 8vo. 1858.. 4 00
HAMILTON'S PHILOSOPHY. Edited by the translator of Cousin's Works.. 1 50
THE RISE AND PROGRESS OF THE ENGLISH CONSTITUTION. By E. S. Creasy, M. A., Barrister at Law, Prof. of History in University College, London, Law Fellow of King's College, Cambridge. Third edition, revised, with additions. 12mo. 349 pages.. 1 00
SCHWEGLER'S HISTORY OF PHILOSOPHY. Translated by Julius Seelye 1 25
WINSLOW'S ELEMENTS OF MORAL PHILOSOPHY..................... 1 25
WILSON'S ELEMENTARY TREATISE ON LOGIC........................ 1 25
TAPPAN'S ELEMENTS OF LOGIC.. 1 00
JOHNSON, ON THE MEANING OF WORDS. 1 vol., 12mo. Cloth........ 1 00

FRENCH.

OLLENDORFF'S FIRST LESSONS IN FRENCH. By G. W. Greene....... $ 50
" NEW METHOD OF LEARNING FRENCH. By J. L. Jewett.. 1 00
OLLENDORFF'S NEW METHOD OF LEARNING FRENCH. By V. Value 1 00
" COMPANION TO FRENCH GRAMMAR. By G W. Greene 75
ANDREWS AND BATCHELOR'S NEW AND COMPREHENSIVE FRENCH INSTRUCTOR.. 1 25
ANDREWS AND BATCHELOR'S PRACTICAL PRONOUNCER AND KEY TO INSTRUCTOR.. 1 00
SIMONNE'S TREATISE ON FRENCH VERBS............................ 50
BADOIS' GRAMMAR FOR FRENCHMEN TO LEARN ENGLISH........ 1 00
SPIERS AND SURENNE'S STANDARD PRONOUNCING FRENCH & ENGLISH AND ENGLISH & FRENCH DICTIONARY. Edited by G. P. Quackenbos, A. M. 1 large vol., 8vo. 1400 pages.................. 3 00
ABRIDGMENT OF THE ABOVE. New edition, large type, 12mo. 973 pp.. 1 50
SURENNE'S FRENCH AND ENGLISH PRONOUNCING DICTIONARY. Pocket edition.. 90
DE FIVAS' ELEMENTARY FRENCH READER........................... 50
" CLASSIC FRENCH READER........................... 1 00
ROEMER'S FIRST FRENCH READER.................................... 1 00
" SECOND FRENCH READER.................................... 1 25

ROEMER'S POLYGLOT READER—FRENCH	$1 00
ROWAN'S MODERN FRENCH READER	75
COLLOT'S DRAMATIC FRENCH READER	1 00
COUTAN'S SELECTION OF FRENCH POETRY	1 00
THE NEW TESTAMENT. Edited by J. F. Ostervald	56
COMMENT ON PARLE FRANÇAIS À PARIS. A New Guide for learning French as spoken in Paris	50
VOLTAIRE'S HISTORY OF CHARLES XII. By Surenne	50
FÉNÉLON'S TÉLÉMAQUE. Edited by Surenne	50
CHOUQUET'S FRENCH CONVERSATIONS AND DIALOGUES	50
" YOUNG LADIES' GUIDE TO FRENCH COMPOSITION	"
SURENNE'S FRENCH MANUAL AND TRAVELLER'S COMPANION	62

SPANISH.

OLLENDORFF'S NEW METHOD OF LEARNING SPANISH. By Velazquez	$1 00
DE VERE'S GRAMMAR OF THE SPANISH LANGUAGE. With Exercises	1 00
OLLENDORFF'S GRAMMAR FOR SPANIARDS TO LEARN FRENCH. By Simonne	2 00
OLLENDORFF'S GRAMMAR FOR SPANIARDS TO LEARN ENGLISH	2 00
SEOANE, NEUMAN, AND BARETTI'S SPANISH & ENGLISH AND ENGLISH & SPANISH DICTIONARY	5 00
ABRIDGMENT OF THE ABOVE	1 50
BUTLER'S SPANISH TEACHER	50
VELAZQUEZ' SPANISH PHRASE-BOOK	38
TOLON'S ELEMENTARY SPANISH READER	63
VELAZQUEZ' NEW SPANISH READER	1 25
ROEMER'S POLYGLOT READER—SPANISH	1 00
MORALES' PROGRESSIVE SPANISH READER	1 00
DON QUIXOTE. A revised edition (in English)	2 00
In Spanish, 12mo., 695 pages	1 25

GERMAN.

OLLENDORFF'S NEW METHOD OF LEARNING GERMAN. Edited by G. J. Adler	$1 00
EICHHORN'S PRACTICAL GERMAN GRAMMAR	1 00
OLLENDORFF'S NEW GRAMMAR FOR GERMANS TO LEARN THE ENGLISH LANGUAGE. By P. Gands	1 00
BRYAN'S GRAMMAR FOR GERMANS TO LEARN ENGLISH	75
ADLER'S GERMAN & ENGLISH AND ENGLISH & GERMAN DICTIONARY	5 50
ADLER'S ABRIDGED GERMAN & ENGLISH AND ENGLISH & GERMAN DICTIONARY	1 50
ADLER'S PROGRESSIVE GERMAN READER	1 00
OEHLSCHLAGER'S PRONOUNCING GERMAN READER	1 00
ROEMER'S POLYGLOT READER—GERMAN	1 00
ADLER'S HAND-BOOK OF GERMAN LITERATURE	1 50
HEYDENREICH'S ELEMENTARY GERMAN READER	50

ITALIAN.

OLLENDORFF'S PRIMARY LESSONS.................................. $ 50
" NEW METHOD OF LEARNING ITALIAN,.............. 75
BARETTI'S ITALIAN AND ENGLISH DICTIONARY. Revised, enlarged, and improved. By Davenport and Comelati. 2 large vols., 8vo. Cloth... 7 50
FORESTI'S ITALIAN READER.................................. 1 00
ROEMER'S POLYGLOT READER—ITALIAN.................................. 1 00

LATIN.

ARNOLD'S FIRST AND SECOND LATIN BOOK AND PRACTICAL GRAMMAR. By Spencer.................................. $ 75
ARNOLD'S FIRST LATIN BOOK. By Harkness.................................. 75
HARKNESS' SECOND LATIN BOOK AND READER.................................. 90
ARNOLD'S LATIN PROSE COMPOSITION.................................. 1 00
" CORNELIUS NEPOS. With Notes.................................. 1 00
BEZA'S LATIN TESTAMENT.................................. 75
CÆSAR'S COMMENTARIES. Notes by Spencer.................................. 1 00
CICERO DE OFFICIIS. Notes by Thatcher.................................. 90
CICERO'S SELECT ORATIONS. Notes by Johnson.................................. 1 00
HORACE. With Notes, &c., by Lincoln.................................. 1 25
TACITUS' HISTORIES. Notes by Tyler.................................. 1 25
" GERMANIA AND AGRICOLA. Notes by Tyler.................................. 1 25
SALLUST. With Notes by Prof. Butler.................................. 1 00
LIVY. With Notes, &c., by Lincoln. Map.................................. 1 00
QUINTUS CURTIUS: Life and Exploits of Alexander the Great. Edited and illustrated with English Notes, by Prof. Crosby.................................. 1 00

GREEK.

CHAMPLIN'S SHORT AND COMPREHENSIVE GREEK GRAMMAR..... $ 75
KUHNER'S ELEMENTARY GREEK GRAMMAR.................................. 1 50
KENDRICK'S GREEK OLLENDORFF.................................. 1 00
ARNOLD'S FIRST GREEK BOOK.................................. 75
" GREEK PROSE COMPOSITION. Edited by J. A. Spencer...... 75
" SECOND GREEK PROSE COMPOSITION. Edited by Spencer 75
" GREEK READING BOOK. Edited by Spencer.................................. 1 25
BOISE'S EXERCISES IN GREEK PROSE COMPOSITION.................................. 75
HERODOTUS. With Notes by Prof. Johnson.................................. 75
XENOPHON'S MEMORABILIA OF SOCRATES. Notes by Prof. Robbins.. 1 00
" ANABASIS. Edited, with Notes, by Prof. Boise.................................. 1 00
SOPHOCLES' ŒDIPUS TYRANNUS. Notes by Prof. Crosby.................................. 75

SYRIAC

UHLEMANN'S SYRIAC GRAMMAR. Translated from the German, by Enoch Hutchinson. With a Course of Exercises in Syriac Grammar, a Chrestomathy, and brief Lexicon, prepared by the translator.................................. $3 50

HEBREW.

GESENIUS' HEBREW GRAMMAR. Edited by Rödiger. Translated from the last German Edition, by Conant. 8vo.................................. $1 5[illegible]

www.ingramcontent.com/pod-product-compliance
Lightning Source LLC
LaVergne TN
LVHW010252110826
845151LV00004B/1448

* 9 7 8 1 4 2 5 5 2 4 0 0 5 *